Love of Life

The Kingdom Way

Copyright © 2020 Ogeyi.

All Scripture quotations, unless otherwise indicated, are taken from the Holy Bible, New Revised Standard Version®, NRSV® Copyright © 1995, 1996, 1998, 2014 by Biblica, Inc.™ Used by permission of Zondervan. All rights reserved worldwide. www.zondervan.com. The "NRSV" and "New Revised Standard Version" are trademarks registered in the United States Patent and Trademark Office by Biblica, Inc.™

All art by Ogeyi.

Dedication

May your light illuminate your divine assignment.

Table of Contents

Life

The Musicality of Life 1

Calling 4

7 Deadly Sins Vs. 7 Lively Virtues 10

Belief Systems 17

    Test the Waters 23

    The Dangers of Low Self-Esteem & Insecurity 24

    People Pleaser 25

    Control Freaks 28

    7 Signs of a Trauma Bonded Relationship 36

    Love Language Abuse 52

        Quality Time 53

        Physical Touch 55

        Words of Affirmation 56

        Gifts 59

        Acts of Service 61

Principles 63

    Lion & Lioness 7 Roars of Conduct 65

    Lions Creed 66

Essence

Mind, Body, Spirit, Soul 69
    Mind Wealth 72
    Body Wealth 80
    Spirit Wealth 90
        Bonds 91
        Spiritual Warfare 93
    Soul Wealth 94

Narcissism 97
    Results of Narcissism 99
    The Unicorn & The Pegasus 100
    Cerebral Narcissist 116
    Somatic Narcissist 117

Love

True Love Never Ends 121

    The One 128

    Love vs In Love 131

Love is not Earned 137

Unequally Yoked Equals Getting Choked 143

Be Neither Master Nor Slave 151

Be Emotionally and Spiritually Wealthy 159

Make it, Don't Fake it 165

Relationships Are Like Jobs, Produce Good Fruit 171

Kingdom Discernment

Walk in Faith and Not Fear of Culture 207
Rescue Dog and Sitting Duck Syndrome 213
    Rescue Dog Syndrome 213
    Sitting Duck Syndrome 215
Tales from the Negaverse 221
Do You Love Who You Have to Be? 233
What, When, Why, How? 241
Tax Return Love 249
The Roses 253
Conclusion 257

Allowing yourself to fall in love... feels like your world is caving inside itself, and you have no desire to save yourself. It affects the atmosphere, how you process your instincts... enhances, enchants your desires. Your sense of time is reflective of the length of a dream; when you sleep. A mute interruption of sound transitioning to an unexpected tune you subconsciously chose to accept. Love is the only maddening thing universally celebrated and accepted that threatens to challenge your survival instincts. May you guide your life not by the death of your heart, but by the depth of your resurrection.

"Where must we go, we who wander this Wasteland, in search of our better selves?"

-The First History Man

The Musicality of Life

Each sin has an opposing virtue. When healing from a vice it's important to step in the right direction into a virtue. Each virtue has a love language attached to it. Knowing your love language is important in understanding how you are fulfilled. If your love language is not nurtured with your virtues, it's hard to have a fulfilling life.

Life has a series of pleasures and difficulties. What matters is not necessarily the difficulty level; it's the payoff. The best relationships are not only fulfilling, they are fruitful and add to your life rather than subtract from it. When you think of a life well-lived, you should think of it as a movie. The best movies have a great story line and a great score. In unison, the story line and music should have a heavenly harmony that makes us rise to our own excellence.

"I live, I die, I live again."

-Nux Mad Max: Fury Road

Life is a series of blessings and lessons. Your authentic self lives in your virtues and dies in your vices. The translation for sin is "to miss the mark." Pay attention to the music you listen to. The truth of your current essence resonates with the melodies of your heart. If you were to create your own track where do you stand? Do the lyrics match the background music? Does it resonate with the person you want to become? In order to miss the mark, you must have a target. If you are hitting the target you should be fulfilled. If not, you need to deduce where you went wrong. Is the problem the target itself, or the broken arrow of your way of thinking? What lies have you been telling yourself?

With this book, I will help you uncover your own theme song and help you rise to your higher self. Your higher self is who God called you to be. Your inner lion or lioness will prowl to the theme song of its own authentic heartbeat. We as human beings were created in the Fall (Adam and Eve); however, it's important to rise in virtue. Life is a journey to live authentically in harmony with your highest self.

Love of Life

Calling

"Ask, and it will be given to you; search, and you will find; knock, and the door will be opened for you."
(Matthew 7:7)

  Before you ask, before you knock, surrender. Our hearts are not always pure, and to live in harmony with the divine, we must seek truth and seek God. We often desire what is not good or not right for us. If we do not break free from our sins, we will remain broken and vacuous, adding to the chaos of this world. Surrender your previous ways, your previous wills, and adhere to God's way and His will. You are to call on God, and God will call you. Many people call on God, but they do not hear or answer the phone when he calls. Some people treat God as a genie that is supposed to grant all their wishes. This is deceptive and untrue. If you do not have a relationship with the Lord, do not expect the benefits of the Kingdom.

  God wants a relationship with every single one of us, but it is our free will and choice to choose Him. If you desire to have a relationship, isolate yourself to get focused. Read the Bible, repent, say your prayers and have conversations with God and see what happens in your life. God may speak through what you hear, see, or dream of it all depends on the individual and their

relationship. It is crucial to have your own personal relationship. If you ask God to reveal Himself to you, He will in due time. When you are obedient and follow your calling, He will create a path unforeseen due to your faith.

How you spend your time is vital. Seek and you shall find. Gods' will and God's way calls us to do our best, and we can fight and resist it if we so choose. In our resistance is chaos that leads to pain, which often happens when we do not trust and believe in God. This is not to say God's will faces no challenges. The turmoil you may face following God's will, leads to peace eventually as long as you trust in Him. There is lots of noise and distraction in the world. Non-believers may look at, how Christians behave and think their behaviors are strange, weird, corrupt, or bad. Just because someone says they are a believer doesn't mean they are a follower. Even if they follow, they may do so and stumble due to imperfection.

You should not expect perfection from anyone. Non-believers may follow some of God's ways and not believe in Him. However, without clarity of God, faith, and obedience does not make sense. God will give you the desires of your heart once your heart is surrendered to Him. He will renew your heart, your mind, your spirit, and enrich your soul if you fully follow and trust him.

Love of Life

Living our calling is an act of service to God. God calls every single one of us, but it is up to us to pick up the phone. Without the relationship, you will be disconnected from your calling. There is a yearning within all of us to be connected. Not everyone is taught how to hear God's voice. To hear His voice, you must spend quality time with God. That quality time is in prayer, and reading your Bible.

Find a community of believers for support, but above all develop your own personal connection. Human beings will fall and disappoint you, and you will fall and disappoint other people. Always do your best so you can be at rest with what you have done. Always be direct with God, everyone is on their own journey and not everyone is perfect in spirit. God tells each and every one of us our own personal messages and these may not make sense to everybody. It will be your song, at your rhythm, on your time. You must align with God's mark and your own authenticity.

The seven deadly sins and the seven virtues are good places to start looking to see if you are missing the mark. If you are not wary of the consequences of your sins, then you are truly not awake, and if you twist reality it will snap and hurt you beyond imagining. Be aware, be honest, and get ready. You can play into your sins or play into your virtues to try to achieve happiness. Pleasure from sin turns into pain, and it is a hard stain to remove

from the heart. Impure happiness leads to regression. Like a broken record repeating itself, it replays a lesson that has yet to be learned. Impure happiness stunts your growth, leads to immaturity, and impurity. All of which will be a detriment to your self-esteem, and your walk with the Lord. One can get stuck and not progress with the song one is supposed to play in life.

Pure happiness leads to progression and we should enjoy it on time and not fast-forward through it. We only stop learning and growing when we die. It's better to seek to be good than it is to just seek happiness. When we are down, we may spiral into our vices, so we must choose to climb into our virtues. It's better to climb than to face a fall. I will discuss self-love, romantic relationships, and tools of discernment with God's will and way. We all have sinned, and God gives us an opportunity to choose Him, repent, and renew our minds.

In Christianity sins are not rated in terms of which sin is worse; however, humans have a nature within them to decide which sin is worse for them. For most people what determines which sin is worse is the ability to commit said sin in the first place - the impact, and the reversibility of it. For the sake of this book, we will focus on the seven deadly sins and the seven lively virtues in parallel with our love languages. If we do not have fear and love of God, we will create fear and love of idols that are not our creator. The things of this world will not fully

Love of Life

satisfy us. Which would you rather play into - your sins or your virtues? There is power in discipline, and delayed gratification has great rewards. The devil loves instant gratification, and long-term pain. Good tends to operate in long-term peace. In taking responsibility for your life, you will be on your way to finding meaning in your life.

> *"Who saved us and called us with a holy calling, not according to our works but according to his own purpose and grace"*
> *(2 Timothy 1:9)*

Seven Lion & Lioness Love Lessons

7 Deadly Sins Vs. 7 Lively Virtues

Love of Life

7 Deadly Sins (Vices)	7 Lively Virtues
Lust Fornication, Uncontrolled sexual desire Dante's Inferno Explanation: "Excessive love for others."	**Chastity** Purity, Abstinence, Virginity "For this is the will of God, your sanctification: that you abstain from fornication; that each one of you know how to control your own body." (1 Thessalonians 4: 3-5)

Seven Deadly Sins and Seven Lively Virtues

Gluttony	Temperance
Excessive eating and drinking	Humanity, Equanimity, Stability, Moderation
Dante's Inferno Explanation: "Excessive love of pleasure."	"Do not be among winebibbers, or among gluttonous eaters of meat; for the drunkard and the glutton will come to poverty, and drowsiness will clothe them with rags." (Proverbs 23: 20-21)
Greed	**Charity**
Excessive desire for wealth and possessions	Will, Benevolence, Generosity, Sacrifice
Dante's Inferno Explanation: "Love of Money and Power."	"If you offer your food to the hungry and satisfy the needs of the afflicted, then your light shall rise in the darkness and your glow be like the noonday." (Isaiah 58:10)

Love of Life

WARNING

Sloth	Indifference	Diligence
Laziness, Idleness	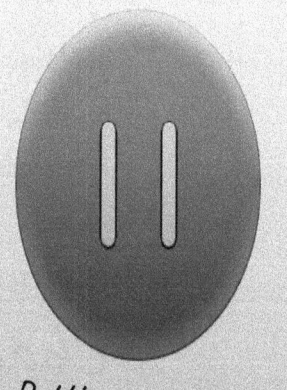 Putting a pause on your life can be a silent killer.	Persistence, Effort
Dante's Inferno Explanation: "Failure to love God with all your heart, all your mind, and all your soul."		"From the fruit of the mouth one is filled with good things, and manual labor has its reward." (Proverbs 12:14)

    This sin and this virtue are the most critical in your calling. We all make mistakes and at least with some bad we can make good out of it later. If we are not making anything, then we have nothing to work with, and by having nothing to work with we cannot render meaning into our lives.

Seven Deadly Sins and Seven Lively Virtues

Wrath Anger, Hate Dante's Inferno Explanation: "Love of justice perverted to revenge and spite."	**Patience** Forgiveness, Mercy "So let us not grow weary in doing what is right, for we will reap at harvest time, if we do not give up." (Galatians 6:9)
Envy Jealousy, Discontent Dante's Inferno Explanation: "Love of your own good perverted to a desire to deprive other men of theirs."	**Kindness** Satisfaction, Compassion "But love your enemies, do good and lend, expecting nothing in return. Your reward will be great, and you will be children of the most high; for he is kind to the ungrateful and the wicked." (Luke 6:35)

Love of Life

The Devils Way

Vs

God's

Pride	Humility
Proud, Vain	Bravery, Deep Respect
Dante's Explanation: "Love of self perverted to hatred and contempt for your neighbor."	"For by the grace given to me I say to everyone among you not to think of yourself more highly than you out to think, but to think with sober judgment, each according to the measure of faith that God has assigned." (Romans 12:3)

Seven Deadly Sins and Seven Lively Virtues

Behavior Results	
Sin (Impure Happiness)	Virtue (Pure Happiness)
Destroy Vacuous Satisfaction	Nurture Fulfilling growth
Downwards direction of stairs to meet the lower self. Pathway to pain.	Forward direction of stairs to meet your higher self. Pathway to peace.

"For we know that the law is spiritual; but I am of the flesh, sold into slavery under sin. I do not understand my own actions. For I do not do what I want, but I do the very thing I hate."

(Romans 7:14-15)

Love of Life

Always remember, people do what they want to do and or what they feel they have to do. What they feel they have to do may be a lie, and what they want to do may not always be lived truthfully. If you do not master what you want to do, in alignment with what you feel you have to do in your calling, you will be stuck with noise, distractions, and unfruitful attractions.

Not all happiness will make you good, not all goodness will make you happy, but truth with good will set you right, and delight in what is right; will create peace and not pain.

"The coming of the lawless one is apparent in the working of Satan, who uses all power, signs, lying wonders, and every kind of wicked deception for those who are perishing, because they refused to love the truth and be saved. For this reason God sends them a powerful delusion leading them to believe what is false, so that all who have not believed the truth but took pleasure in unrighteousness will be condemned."
(2 Thessalonians 2:9-12)

Belief Systems

"I consider that the sufferings of this present time are not worth comparing with the glory about to be revealed to us."
(Romans 8:18)

    Whatever gets to you first in terms of information, and experience will be your baseline. Your baseline will be your reference point to check in to reality. Whatever is first usually has the most influential power. Baseline helps you understand form and structure, the same way your first language helps you form sentences. The new language you learn will always reference your first one, and you will orient your understanding based on your original process of learning.

    Think about your first barber or hairstylist. Whoever did your hair regularly first, set the standard and framework for how you thought the procedure should go. Another person may do it differently and you may perceive the new way as weird, better, worse, or just different depending on how you feel about the result. Perhaps the hairstylist you saw before never massaged the scalp and said you were supposed to itch after every appointment. If you have not tried anything else you will assume it as part of the process and not know any better. After all, it was likely a parent who took you there, someone you trusted to know better. Your self-esteem was primarily developed by the warmth and care of your parents.

Not all that is routine is right or best suited for you. Your baseline does not have to be part of your authenticity. What you may consider parts of your personality, may just be blockers that are not allowing you to tap into your full potential. You may consider yourself shy when your excellence is just dormant and not yet awakened. You may say you aren't a phone person when really, you just fear vulnerability and connection and would love the phone if they could get past your insecurities. Your pain is not your personality.

Your pain cloaks you, and your peace soaks you in the authenticity of your soul. Before you say "that's just my personality," or worse, have someone else tell you "that's just your personality," ask yourself if it is authentic and serving your higher self. Insecurity is not an identity trait, it's a state of being. Moods are states of being that fluctuate and your character should not fluctuate. Feelings may come and go. If your state of being is irrational and not serving you it should be eradicated and dealt with. If it isn't authentic or serving your higher self, consider it an element of yourself that you should wrestle with into serving you rather than enslaving you.

There is a baseline of human behavior and the hardwiring in each individual may vary. Wires may get

Belief Systems

tangled, and affect output(giving) and input (receiving) when it comes to perception. Mangled wires do not represent who you are - it represents your dysfunction. Show the world who you are, and let it speak for itself. If you let the world tell you who you are, you will likely delude yourself into mediocrity or whatever is functional to the outside world. Check the default of your baseline - it may not be true or optimal to your best self. The information you received first may not be true, and if it is not true then there is no need to be loyal to it.

Familiarity creates comfort. Even a red flag may appear soothing to someone if it represents home to them. Chaos can look like stability if it is what you are most familiar with. In that case; clarity with truth and goodness will seem strange and uncomfortable. Comfortability doesn't always mean right; it could simply mean familiar. Being comfortable can be far more dangerous than being risky. If you are going to heal from a painful past you have to make your past feel foreign to you. You have to make the future you desire familiar to you.

Instant gratification can rot your works and leave you underdeveloped. It may be sweet like candy but may rot your tooth you need to eat broccoli. When what we want doesn't always serve our good, we must starve ourselves from the bad we are consuming, in that process one will begin to shift to acquire a new palette that is ultimately fulfilling. Essentially, if you are driven by purpose, then you will be consistent in works and delay gratification. However, if you instead you are focused on feeling good then your behavior will lean towards things that provide instant gratification.

God may bless us all in mysterious ways. However, there is a reason why lottery winners usually end up broke later. Their fruits were not a reward of discipline, their fruits were handed to them by chance. If one depends on chance, they will feel helpless because chance is not easy to replicate or control. Lacking control leads to a lack of power to do good or receive good. The more good options you have the less likely you are to fall.

There are three positions in life: leader, follower, or rogue. A rogue neither follows or leads anyone; they go on their own, and occasionally become incidental leaders, or incidental followers to the plan they have in life. They operate alone. It is important that before a man becomes a leader to his wife that he goes on a rogue mission to discover and develop himself. Being solid in your identity and having a relationship with Christ helps you orient direction. You should find where you want to go before you serve other people.

Going on your rogue mission is the only way to be certain that you have the strength and fortitude to distinctly do things through your authenticity and

Belief Systems

relationship with God. It is important that a woman goes rogue as well and learns to lead in her own strengths and learns to serve a leader as well. A declaration of independence should come before interdependence in relationships.

You will fail along the way of your journey in life, and you will win. True champions do not judge their losses as final conclusions of their character and their abilities. Admirable people give themselves another chance and keep the possibility that faith can be evidently true by virtue of the fruit of the spirit put into the seeds of work. Despite all odds, they focus on fulfilling a purpose. Hope in works with fruits not yet seen is faith.

Imagine going to the beach and being stung by a jellyfish. Some stings are not that bad, and others can be traumatizing, or lethal. You may not ever want to go into the ocean again. You may say you prefer the land, due to fear of the sea and not love of the land. If all you've known of the sea is pain, it is hard to see the possibility of gain. Some of the best treasures are in the sea and it is a tragedy to have never known it.

"Desire without knowledge is not good, and one who moves too hurriedly misses the way."
Proverbs (19:2)

The sand represents familiarity and may appear safe simply because you know it. Even if all you've known

of sand is pain, it doesn't scare you because it is familiar. Any dangerous animal on land is the devil you know, and in the sea may be the devil you don't know. There is beauty on land, and beauty in the sea. At heart, we can live on land or at sea. You cannot be fully developed and actualized without the exploration of the unknown.

A lot of people won't leave their abusers because they are used to them. Like a bad habit, they don't know how to break it because it's all they know. They are conditioned to show up at their house at a certain time etc. They can tell you how much they hate the person and then call them afterward and act as if everything is okay. Routine becomes subconscious, and you have to consciously be aware and stop yourself.

On gossip websites there once was a trend to be the first commenter to write "first". Evil knows the power of being the first one. It's petty, it's immature, but there is power in infiltrating and setting the framework. Think about people who have worked at the same job for ten years. You can put them in a new job and they will naturally do their old procedures out of habit until you teach them the new baseline. However, to follow new habits, you may now need to kill some old ones. What is familial is what is on land, the land represents your family and the baseline of what you know. The sea is the unknown.

Belief Systems

Test the Waters

But ask in faith, never doubting, for the one who doubts is like a wave of the sea, driven and tossed by the wind; for the doubter, being double-minded and unstable in every way, must not expect to receive anything from the Lord.
(James 1:6-8)

People achieve false love all the time. They glorify it as real love and fulfillment, and some may say time will tell. However, it is telling all the time, but it's just a matter of volume and actual listening if you can hear it. It is in the frequency and not everyone has good hearing or listening skills. What's the musicality? Are the lyrics beautiful but the background music dreary? Is the background music wonderful but the lyrics questionable? Sometimes, they are out of sync and resonating at a low frequency that is hard for others to comprehend or understand. Not everyone is aware, and not everyone knows what true love is.

Double-minded people try to pick the best of both worlds. Indecisiveness showcases fragility in character. You build a solid mind when you have solid principles rooted in your identity. Without our identity, all we have to operate from are our moods and influences from others. Moods and influences are dangerous without principles because it will cost you your character. Your

character is vital and your identity in Christ should not shift so easily at will. When it comes to healing, it's best to be honest, and then be good, as opposed to just being "positive." Test the temperature level and the toxicity of the water. Is it hot or cold? Pure or contaminated?

The Dangers of Low Self-Esteem & Insecurity

Knowing your worth is not a matter of currency. It's not a rating system that fluctuates. You should not think you are superior or inferior to anyone. Target aligning with your higher self and don't judge your worth by those around you. The value of a dime fluctuates based on societal value. Instead of a dime piece (a woman who is considered a ten on a scale of 1-10), one should orchestrate themselves as it's a puzzle piece refined by God in our works. True love is not conditional and should not be measured by conditional things such as societal value.

If you do not love yourself, all you will be capable of is obsession and solitary depression. The notion of "I don't like me" will create thoughts and situations that revolve positions to confirm your bias. You will either plead "don't like me" or "please like me," to people you desire to be around. People do not stand up for things

they don't like, and if you do not like yourself you will not stand up for yourself. If you are insecure you are likely to commit to fears and lies, and pain will be your deciding factor over all else. That pain will triumph love for it will distort what love is even as you seek it. Your view on love will be twisted, just as your view on yourself is twisted. Boundaries that should never be crossed, will be crossed and even welcomed at the hands of evil if you do not love yourself. A lot of people who have low self-esteem have had their boundaries violated. Their pain runs so deep that they rather defeat themselves first.

People Pleaser

People pleasers are often created as a reaction from a violation. They usually grew up with their boundaries constantly being violated. People pleasers freeze and appease their violators. Fight, flight, and freeze are trauma responses. The violation could have happened physically, mentally, emotionally, spiritually, and each element could have been combined to tear at the soul. People pleasers usually have an anxious attachment style in their romantic relationship. They are negative about themselves, positive about others, and tend to be clingy in their relationships. An anxiously attached person will need reassurance the relationship will last due to fear of abandonment. They may fight for their relationships but will freeze when they are supposed to leave.

People-pleasing can be a detriment to who you are supposed to become and a detriment to your servitude to God. People pleasers are loyal to nobody, and a slave to the goals of others. They may appear loyal, and may "accidentally" cheat due to feeling the need to appease someone who is down. People pleasers are highly likely to become infatuated; they lack maturity in identity and are childish with their desires. They may even say they deserve the unhealthy behavior of their partner to justify their "unconditional love" which is actually "unconditional infatuation due to unhealed wounds". Soothing an unhealthy craving is sick but will appear healthy due to the release of anxiety during consumption. Satiating an appetite may appear to be angelic in purpose but the devil's in the details in terms of reasoning and logic.

People pleasers trust other people over themselves and sacrifice their happiness for others. They are governed by fear, guilt, and shame. In a sense, they humanize other people and dehumanize themselves. People pleasers have empathy and are not very aggressive and, in their passivity, they cannot always be morally good. A genuinely moral person can do evil or submit to it, they just choose not to. For example, virginity until marriage is a virtue but if it is not by choice, it does

Belief Systems

not merit a celebration of good behavior. People pleasers lack power in their position.

People-pleasing is feminine in energy but is toxic for both males and females. If a woman is a people pleaser, she may want to help but feel helpless and therefore be attracted to a controlling man. If a man is a people pleaser, he may desire to be a leader but not believe in himself and therefore be attracted to a controlling woman who has masculine energy. If he desires to lead, he will not respect and honor her despite the attraction. He will endlessly desire a woman whom he does not think he can compare to due to his lack of belief in himself to lead. People pleasers lack respect and honor for themselves and are very insecure.

7 Traits of a People Pleaser

1. They cloak how they think and feel
2. They exude care for others at their detriment
3. They cannot stand up for themselves
4. They have a problem saying no
5. They don't have healthy boundaries
6. They over-explain or over apologize
7. They have relationships that either earned or familiar only.

Love of Life

"The fear of others lays a snare, but one who trusts in the Lord is secure."
(Proverbs 29:25)

Control Freaks

Control freaks are also created from trauma due to violations. Control freaks tend to try to master people to serve their own selfish goals. When a control freak is violated, they are likely to fight and not trust and therefore dominate. Control freaks do not trust other people and are loyal to themselves. Control freaks only humanize themselves and dehumanize others because they have lack empathy for others. Control freaks usually have an avoidant attachment style. A person who has an avoidant attachment will be positive about themselves and negative about others. They are likely to be independent and avoid or downplay problems. They struggle with getting close to people and often have walls up.

The nature of being controlling is masculine and this is toxic no matter which sex possesses it. If a woman is a control freak, she may lead with masculine energy. She may desire a man who is a good leader, but not trust a man will lead in a way she can honor and respect - and therefore end up with an effeminate man. If the woman leading desires to be a helper and not a leader, she will

not respect or want to honor the man she is with and will therefore resent him.

A man of honor is masculine, a woman of grace is feminine. Grace and Honor have humility, and lacking humility leads to pride or lowliness. If a man is a control freak, he may desire a helper but may not trust a woman to help him and therefore be attracted to a woman who would appear to be a helpless people pleaser. He too will not honor or respect the people pleaser. Part of honor and respect entails freedom and admiration. Your partner has to admire your choices, and see that you made a distinct choice in your power and not by default of your ability. Control freaks typically have a lot of pride.

A man who is a control freak is dangerous to a woman; a woman who is a people pleaser is dangerous to herself. A woman who is a control freak is dangerous to a man's manhood; a man who is a people pleaser is a danger to his self-worth. Either way, being a control freak or a people pleaser is harmful whether you are a male or female. It causes hurt and damage in different ways. People pleasers and control freaks are both broken and are compatible with their dysfunction. They are a diabolical match.

People pleasers believe in others, and not themselves. Control freaks believe in themselves, and not others. People pleasers lack willpower, and control freaks will power over them. Masculine and feminine energies

Love of Life

match and create synergy. People-pleasing is a result of a helper being dysfunctional, and being controlling is a form of a leader being dysfunctional. People pleasers and control freaks may be attracted to each other; however, when you heal the desire to bond breaks.

We are all beautifully and wonderfully made in the eyes of God, and believing otherwise is a lie that welcomes the devil to play with your mind. When someone has low self-esteem, they are likely to compromise all the things God has in store for them. They are likely to lie and negate good things. Low self-esteem will breed lies that go against your design. If you are a male and your self-esteem is shot you might become more feminine. If you are a woman and your self-esteem is shot you may become more masculine. Either way you will lead with cowardice over prowess or corrupt prowess in a savage way. Unfortunately, the desire to control someone or to appease them increases the chances of them lying to you and themselves. The reason for this is because both focus on results as their goals, and are motivated by bad character (control freak) and low self-worth (people pleaser).

A people pleaser can covertly only please themselves, and therefore be a shy controller. They can appear to help you and slowly destroy you at the same time. That shy controller is likely covertly narcissistic and will be the hardest to identify in terms of brokenness and

Belief Systems

might be the most dangerous due to their ability to cause damage while not being detected. An overt abuser will spill water on you, a covert abuser will slip a drug into your drink. It will take a while to detect and will be difficult to trace.

When the people pleaser (who is anxiously attached) fights, the control freak (who is avoidantly attached) will coldly flight or freeze. When the people pleasure tries to flee or flight, the control freak will fight. This makes them a diabolical heart-breaking match that is unhealthy and detrimental to both sides. The people pleaser is hungry and wary, the control freak is in denial of their own hunger. In a way, the people pleaser admires that denial and wish they had it. Their wish is a false dream and a seed in destruction of a fruitful life. Prepare for fake plants and fake fruits to appear or nothing at all. It will be posed like a fake picture and there will be nothing natural or organic about it.

A man who lacks ambition, and has low self-esteem is dangerous to whomever he bonds with; a woman who lacks the desire to help and has low self-esteem is dangerous to whomever she bonds with. When you are empty and low on esteem you will be full of selfishness and become dependent on others for validation. There is no such thing as a dependent person who is mature without ailment. A dependent person who is supposed to be mature takes advantage of people or gets taken advantage of. Those that take advantage are masters, and those getting taken advantage of are slaves. Two people together are supposed to expand together not contract while the other expands. If both expand as one, they will thrive together.

You should not enable the false identity but heal from the very force that made you switch positions and directions. Justifying illusions in the placement of the truth will not bring true peace, it will bring true chaos. If you have to justify something, you should probably let it go. If something is good there is no need to justify it. Anytime we go against our inherent design we go against our development and therefore cause destruction.

It's crucial not to lie to yourself about being wonderfully made in the image of God. Low self-esteem will put you in a state that leads to desperation and unhappiness, which leads to a lack of discernment and poor decision making. The truth is like water it will quench your thirst for knowledge but if it is false it will not nourish you. In rejecting water, you may drink soda or another substance and claim to be "just as good" or – as "fine" as water. After all, soda is a liquid and even toxins may have water.

The placebo effect of the false illusion will eventually take its toll and expose the truth, and

Belief Systems

dehydration won't put you in a state of alignment for excellence in goodness. The nutrients of the fruits you plant in your mind will be reaped as you sowed them. Not every fruit is perfect and 100 percent dirt-free, but it should enhance your life, and not take from it.

"On the last day of the festival, the great day, while Jesus was standing there, he cried out, "Let anyone who is thirsty come to me, and let the one who believes in me drink. As the scripture has said, Out of the believer's heart shall flow rivers of living water.""
(John 7:37)

Insecurity breeds fear and activates survival mode. Survival mode will make you selfish. An insecure person cannot love for they are led by fear of what they do not have. The hunger, famine, will breed desperation deep enough to justify the consumption of toxins. An insecure person will create narratives that support lies and negativity. Insecurity creates a primal mode of thinking in a counterproductive way.

People are like food, and everyone has a palate. People who are picky eaters are often picky about who they choose to date. Being a picky eater can be good or bad depending on the wellness of your palate. Not being picky can expose you to anything whether it is good or bad. Your palate will be based on your exposure, desire, and management skills. If you cannot appreciate a good

person, like you would a good meal, do not keep them. We all deserve to be desired for the goodness we have, and it isn't fair to that individual or others who can appreciate them.

What you devour may be due to proximity and belief in ability to capture what you desire. Instead of thriving, you will be surviving simply to get through to the next meal of the day. If you do not see anything good that you want, then go on a fast and change location. God is like water and you can survive on that for days to come, and in that fast, you will gain clarity and direction to the food you need. Insecurity creates a scarcity mindset that allows you to settle in comfortably into the wrong relationships. Insecurity will create impatience to wait on God's will and way. Once you are secure and not insecure, you can healthily give to others.

Obsession and addiction should not be confused with love and stability. Obsession is a sick form of trying to create stability. Obsession should be deemed as childish love in that you feel it intensely for nonsensical reasons. Addiction is a sick bond disguised as a connection to love. Many people think in terms of what you want vs what you need. If a person fulfills a need that you should be filling yourself you run the risk of being dependent on them. A person who surrenders their power cannot be trusted to do well for what they desire. Thoughts such as "I cannot live without you," and "I don't

Belief Systems

know who I would be without you," are often romanticized but such thoughts are signs of an unhealthy relationship.

Obsession is bred through a lack of security in fulfillment. You may pick a sin and get addicted to it while trying to construct "a new reality" via fantasy. That fantasy will inevitably deconstruct your identity while trying to sustain oneself through a false dream of security. We all get an itch to satiate a desire and fixation rather than true focus will be at play when we are not healthy. Satiating an itch can give us pleasure or give us pain, and if it gives us both it is scaring, and if it gives us peace it is renewing to the skin of our being blemish-free. Life is bound to have some scuffs and burns. The goal is not perfection, the goal is production and growth. Perfectionism can be stifling, and a harsh judge of character stands still or regresses. How fruitful is the ground you walk on without nurtured seeds?

When someone obsesses, their identity is surrendered to whatever force they have selected. Insecure people are desperate for security which is the perfect formula for obsession. Insecurity stems from low self-esteem and instability. Love and stability are necessary to have pure happiness. We all hunger and thirst in life but when we starve, we create a new monster that tends to lack humanity if we do not have good character. Insecure people with low self-esteem will tend to make fear-based decisions, stunting their growth. The

Love of Life

good in life will be malnourished, and bad will be replenished by sloth or any of the other deadly sins governed by fear and not love. Love is like a drug in terms of its euphoria but not in its toxins and hangover.

7 Signs of a Trauma Bonded Relationship

1. You break up and make up a lot (Going back and forth is a sign of indecision, lack of desire, or something you lack control over)

2. They feel like an opponent to win over (Feeling like you have to win them sets them apart, and not one with you. Oneness is recognized, not an acquired prize)

3. There is authority, not autonomy in what should be independent decisions (If you need permission for basic needs such as going to the bathroom, eating, sleeping you are in serious danger. If their wish is your command, and your wish is met with silence or avoidance you're in trouble. If you cannot say

Belief Systems

no to them, yet they can say no to you then you have a tyrant, not a partner)

4. Ignoring unhealthy parts of the relationship is key to your survival. (If you are surviving them and not thriving with them you have an unhealthy relationship)

5. Having to hide or sneak around to find the truth or have to hide the truth in fear of irrational behavior.

6. Normal healthy everyday functions cease to be completed or started due to their influence (If your calling in life is starved rather than served due to their influence end the relationship.)

7. Your peace is found in happiness and not goodness for each other (If you have to hurt yourself or hurt them to create peace. If you have to let someone hit you to move forward that's a sign. If you find yourself saying, "As long as their happy, who cares what anyone thinks.")

Love of Life

Self-care and your calling should not be removed for your partner. If your wellness in life is a threat to your partners happiness, you are not with the right person. If someone intentionally hurts you and you feel the need to please them, then you are in a toxic situation. If you do not fix your insecurities and you will feed your vices because your decisions in life will be fear-based and not love-based. A person can feel stuck in a relationship and think it is not right to leave.

A relationship is not a life sentence to make others happy. If one has to live a lie or be deceived by a lie to stay with someone, then the truth is you do not belong together. If you cannot be honest with one another then you do not have a healthy relationship. There are plenty of good people loyal to what's not right for them because they think it is the right thing to do. Lead with truth, then lead with good and do what is right.

If you say things to yourself like "I'm not good enough," you will destroy rather than aid your mission in life because you won't feel worthy. Let's say a woman is very attracted to a man. Imagine that man telling that woman she is beautiful. If she tells him that she is not beautiful she has now insulted that man's vision of beauty. He may try to help her agree with the reality he sees in her. However, that same man may doubt his reality of whether she is beautiful and try to find flaws in her to support the "reality" she presents. He may decide

Belief Systems

telling a woman she is beautiful is a wasted effort and, in the future, may never want to tell another woman she is beautiful again.

Emotional pain can affect everyone even if it is not intentional or direct. Having someone doubt reality is incredibly cruel, and you cannot care for someone if you seduce them untruthfully. The truth should be delivered with kindness and patience, not impatience and wrath. Your intent, actions, and words should all be in alignment with the truth. If it does not match then there is a lie in one, two, or all components.

Where you put your time and energy showcases what you want to grow and what is valuable to you. Many people spend time committed to fear and hatred to the point where they become drained with indifference. Fear and hatred will derail you from your purpose - you will end up with the wrong people doing the wrong things. If you feed fear and negativity, positivity and love will starve. It is not fair to you and it is not the right thing to do. Negativity and fear are not to be ignored and can be dealt with. Energy is a renewable resource but, time is not.

The enemy knows if they can trick you about what is true, and can consume all your time and energy, that you will inevitably give up, and be claimed by them. Watch where you gain energy, and watch where you lose energy. If the enemy has your energy and you see the truth you still may not have the energy to fight back.

Love of Life

Many people are trapped at this stage and surrender to the enemy. When someone does not know the truth they usually respond based upon the energy and conviction of the other person's belief. It is crucial to be strong and hold on to what is true, despite the energy levels and conviction of the person that is opposing them. Otherwise, the enemy will conquer based on energy and deception.

If you want someone to believe something adjust your energy to it truthfully. If you are weak about expressing the truth nobody will be motivated to serve it. Bad can be obvious to some people but not so much to others due to corrupted belief systems. If the devil can corrupt a "good thing" you will not know who to trust, or whether good is possible, and therefore may surrender to evil. The trick is not to shut off your heart to everything, but to align it with God's will and way. The truth should be the basis of where you apply your energy, and it is important to never stop believing in goodness and its ability to conquer evil.

Beware of what you consume, because it may end up consuming you. Your regularly scheduled programming is programming your brain. If you consume things that are not real, they can still have real influence. Do not plant seeds in places you do not want to grow. What you focus on, whether it is good or bad, you will ultimately bond with, and in bonding, there is

Belief Systems

development or detriment to your mind, body, spirit, or soul.

A lot of people will watch reality shows that create a false reality with some real consequences. Dating shows that have narcissistic formulas for "love" are highly revolting for those who have a healthy spirit and mindset. If you enjoy watching people destroying their lives you should ask yourself who hurt you? Even if you know it's not true love, why is watching people lie in the name of love enjoyable?

Keep in mind, just because someone doesn't feel pain doesn't mean they aren't damaged. They may be numb inside or worse dead inside. Everything you consume you will have a relationship with and that relationship will make them part of you. Time is an investment, and it showcases value whether you like it or not. Beware of what you watch, hear, see, and think about. This applies to music, movies, television, etc. Toxic indulgences are the gateway to spiritual warfare.

If you are attracted to things or people who have no nutritional value to add to your life it is time to evaluate your palate and immediately stop consumption. Whether you like eating junk or watching people eat junk there is something off in your humanity for yourself or others. If you have true love or know what true love is, then it hurts to watch other people destroy it, or mock it.

Love of Life

If you are in a relationship and bond over toxic television, food, and or music, remove yourself. There is no such thing as a happy/healthy relationship in which core bonds include toxicity and hatred of self or others. It's best to leave the environment and create a better self than to create a better self within an unhealthy environment. The temptation is not worth your salvation.

You know you have healed when the toxins become a natural repellent and not an attraction. The only way to be able to truly know the difference between good nutrients and bad ingredients is to leave and reorient your mind truthfully. You should treat it like an allergy, test one ingredient at a time and slowly inspect the difference in your life. However, it's best not to filter soda to get water and It's impossible to identify good and bad if you do not know the truth. Knowledge is the power to construct or destroy yourself. If what you know is false you may make a bad thing good or a good thing bad. A bad palate will make excuses and enable bad behaviors and company. Refine your palate by renewing your mind. Is the love you have a false reality and are you utilizing true illusions to justify your inadequacy and lack of fulfillment?

Gary Chapman's book, "The 5 Love Languages," explains the ways people receive and give love. Knowing our love language serves as a reference to discern the difference between a vice and a virtue to lead a fulfilling

Belief Systems

life. It takes discipline to live virtuously. The devil collects undisciplined people because they are prone to fall from grace. The word live spelled backward is evil. Think of vices as moving backward toward evil, and virtue as a way to live. Everyone has their own love language and musicality in which they communicate. We must love ourselves first before we are adequately able to love others.

Self-care helps you to be able to connect with others; self-harm makes you disconnect. Self-harm doesn't always cause pain - it can cause pleasure that creates a lack of connectedness. Lack of connectedness inevitably can create a lack of humanity, which is dangerous. Pure happiness has the power to keep on giving; impure happiness has the power to keep on taking. If you do not know what your language is, think of the times you felt the most loved and look at what language was spoken in those moments. Keep in mind, that the way you project love may not be the same as the way you receive love. Keep in mind you can operate out of self-love or self-hate. Self-love starts with truth, and you must ask yourself if you are operating from peace or operating from pain.

Love of Life

Self-Care		
5 Love Languages	Actions	Virtues
Quality Time "Prepare your work outside, get everything ready for you in the field; and after that build your house." (Proverbs 24:27)	Solitude in things you enjoy, listening to music, watching films, reading books	Temperance
Physical Touch "Do not be wise in your own eyes; fear the Lord, and turn away from evil. It will be healing for your flesh and refreshment for your body." (Proverbs 3:7-8)	Enjoying a cozy blanket, Comfortable footwear, Pampering skincare	Chastity
Gifts "An intelligent mind acquires knowledge, and the ear of the wise seeks knowledge. A gift opens doors; it gives access to the great." (Proverbs 18:15-16)	Buying or creating an item for yourself. Buying clothes, creating artwork.	Charity
Words of Affirmation "Anxiety weighs down the human heart, but a good word cheers it up." (Proverbs 12:25)	Telling yourself good narratives, Writing with joy, Positive reflections	Kindness, Patience

Belief Systems

Acts of Service "Keep your heart with all vigilance, from it flow the springs of life." (Proverbs 4:23) "Before destruction your heart is haughty, but humility goes before honor." (Proverbs 18:12)	Respecting yourself, Cleaning, Exercising, Prayer, Serving God	Humility, Diligence

You cannot love purely without freedom from addiction. Low self-esteem prevents sober judgment. If you pick relationships or other things you want for yourself under the influence, you are likely to make the wrong choices. Think of yourself half asleep with low energy - you are likely to agree to just about anything to return to a state of slumber. You may agree to things you do not want and not realize it until you have a hard awakening. Even upon waking, you must have the energy to avenge yourself. It is nearly impossible to have clarity and act upon your authentic self truthfully when under the toxic spiritual influence of low self-esteem. Eliminate those who encourage or benefit off of your drunkenness. When you insult the goodness you have, you insult God. You are better off not insulting your creator, and building on what you are given.

Self-harm does not always feel bad at the time. It can feel good even upon destruction. There is a desire to

build, and there is a desire to destroy in every single one of us. How we go about it varies with each individual. It has a lot to do with our programming. We are all like computers. We program ourselves based on what we know. We can make any command compute to what we desire it to compute. We can store stuff in our memories, we can put stuff in the recycle bin. Although we delete things there may still be ways to access it just like a computer. Computers can get viruses just as human beings can get viruses. In order to combat corruption, we must have preventative measures and find a cure for what caused us to make mistakes. Sometimes we may need to create firewalls to prevent destruction.

While healing, you need to reprogram yourself to receive true inputs. It is important to orient what is good as good, and what is bad as bad. We are all trying to satisfy a desire. The human condition is prone to have faulty ways. Even when we do things that are wrong on purpose, we are seeking satisfaction in some way. Our yearning is learning along the way as we commit to actions. Our love language can mistranslate bad for good due to a feeling of satisfaction. Think of the sound of a word as opposed to the meaning. The feeling can change simply by the sound and not the meaning of the word. There is a reason people say "that sounds good" or "that does not seem sound to me."

Belief Systems

It is important to know what you are saying and what others are saying as they speak all the different love languages. No matter the feeling behind them, the essence of the truth should be the basis in which we respond and operate from. Not all self-harm hurts, it may just hinder us connecting with others. Here are some ways we can self-harm which leads to disconnect from humanity.

Love of Life

	Self-Harm	
5 Love Languages	Actions	Vice
Quality Time	Overindulgence in solitude, not connecting to others, excessively eating and drinking alone	Gluttony "If you have found honey, eat only enough for you, or else, having too much, you will vomit." (Provers 25:16)
Physical Touch	Indulging in harmful activities for dopamine pleasure (example cutting self), masturbation, indulging in pornography	Lust "Trust in the LORD with all your heart, and do not rely on your own insight. In all your ways acknowledge him, and he will make straight your paths. Do not be wise in your own eyes; fear the LORD, and turn away from evil. It will be healing for your flesh and refreshment for your body." (Proverbs 3:5-8)
Gifts	Buying too much for oneself, only creating for yourself	Greed "Do not withhold good from those to whom it is due, when it is in your power to do it." (Proverbs 3:27)

Belief Systems

Words of Affirmation	Telling yourself bad narratives, Marinating in jealousy of others	Wrath, Envy "A king's anger is like the growling of a lion, but his favor is like dew on the grass." (Proverbs 19:12) "For where there is envy and selfish ambition, there will also be disorder and wickedness of every kind." (James 3:16)
Acts of Service	Loss of self-respect, Uncleanliness, Not exercising, not serving or honoring God's will	Pride, Sloth "Though hatred is covered with guile, the enemy's wickedness will be exposed in the assembly." (Proverbs 26: 26) "Laziness brings on deep sleep; an idle person will suffer hunger." (Proverbs 19:15)

Note that some virtues may not be as attractive to you as others. Is it because of your love language? It is to your advantage to be multilingual in love and to speak multiple love languages. In being multilingual, your understanding of love is not likely to get lost in translation. It's to your advantage to be an effective communicator in the right way. Love languages are not only spoken in romantic relationships, but also in

Love of Life

friendships, families, and the workforce. The workforce is typically limited to words of affirmation, gifts, and acts of service.

Questions to Ask Yourself

1. If I am attached to someone and it is not fulfilling, are my love languages being abused to the point it has impaired my judgment of what is good for me? (vice "goods"). An action in itself can be obviously abusive. However, an act of love can turn into abuse based on the intent of the action.

2. Is the action I am perceiving being utilized to take control (acts of service)?

3. Is the gift I received considerate to my authenticity (gifts)?

4. Is the action a form of abuse of my time (quality time)?

5. Is the positivity genuine or is it a lie (words of affirmation)?

6. Does the action physically hurt and yet is disguised as playful (physical touch)?

7. Is the love given only to receive?

Love is supposed to be free, not costly. This is not to say be cheap with your emotions. This is not to say to

Belief Systems

spend too much. Spending too much at the beginning is love bombing. Love bombing can speak any love language to excess. Real love is about expanding emotional wealth while protecting your assets. If it is costly you are overinvesting which is selfless, if you are taking at someone else's expense you are selfish.

> "Did what is good, then, bring death to me? By no means! It was sin, working death in me through what is good, in order that sin might be shown to be sin, and through the commandment might become sinful beyond measure."
> (Romans 7:13)

Love Language Abuse

Love Language Abuse

Quality Time

Interruption of needs

A person may call you at times when they know you are asleep and this is dishonoring your time. If it is not important or an emergency, then it is inconsiderate. It may feel good for the person who is sleeping to be needed; however, it is an abuse of your time. A selfless person may feel honored to be "needed," but people don't call people they highly respect when they know they are sleeping for something that can wait. A person with a healthy self-esteem will recognize this and find it intolerable. Interrupting healthy habits for nonsensical behavior is not respectful of someone's time.

Isolating you from others

They make you feel special, when in fact it may be a way to control you. If you do not have good counsel behind you, you are not likely to make wise decisions for yourself. Someone can destroy all your previously good relationships. They may even lie to you about other potential friends just so they can keep you to themselves. They may even lie to those potential friends about you so that they have no interest in you. If they are highly manipulative, they may encourage their partner to go

out with others, then summon their partner while they are out just to prove how much power they have asserted over their partner. Or they may text the entire time they are out, and expect them to converse instead of others that they are present with.

There is protectiveness, and then there is control. Protection guards against evil - it is about safety. Control stems from power, it is about maintaining a hostage. The controlling person may say it is about safety, but observe the fruit. Is it rooted in insecurity and evil, or is it rooted in good and providing security? When you have an opponent and not a companion, release yourself from the game they are playing with your heart.

"Whoever isolates himself seeks his own desire; he breaks out against all sound judgment."
(Proverbs 18:1) (ESV)

Love Language Abuse

Physical Touch

Violence

Dopamine signals to the brain that a reward is on its way and physical touch can trigger this. Even if it is in the form of physical abuse, your brain may not know the difference. A healthy sex life is gained through a life that is connected to someone else's pleasure and not only their own. If someone is sexually getting off by abusing you, they are not connected to you; in fact, they are dehumanizing you for their own selfish pleasure. Whether it is physical violence (wrath), or sexual abuse (lust) dehumanization is involved. Sometimes there is no permission which is a clear violation. The selfless may give permission and the selfish will take. Right and wrong are not only about permission, but also about good character in connection to God's will.

"Therefore, do not let sin exercise dominion in your mortal bodies, to make you obey their passions."
(Romans 6:12)

Love of Life

Words of Affirmation

Lying

This love language is abused most often on a casual level. Out of all love languages, this one tends to be the most or least expensive for some people. Some may say they love you to gain permission to do what they want, and some may say because they didn't say "I love you" that they don't have to be held accountable for their actions.

Love is not only in what someone says or does for you... it's the REASON behind it. If someone's words do not match their actions and or intents you cannot trust them. An action can be perceived as a fact and words can be written as a factual statement, but the intent is malleable in perception. If a person's actions, words, and intent do not align consistently there is a subscription in their mind, heart, spirit, or soul to an illusion they may treat as the truth. Somewhere in their being is a lie, and there may be multiple lies, whether these are conscious or unconscious.

A delusional person is not capable of telling the truth. They will live a lie, and allow other people to live a lie around them. When someone is living in truth authentically in harmony with God's will, way, and light, there is alignment. When someone is talking out of

alignment you cannot trust them. They may be lying while they confess what they believe to be the truth.

Regardless of what action they choose, or words they say, the intent they had does not discount accountability. Actions speak louder than words, and the intent (thought) may make a difference, but evidence is the truth you live by. It's good to show and tell. Showing reveals more than telling, and those that lack vulnerability may lack in showing and / or telling. If you lack in showing and telling, then you are living a lie. Be a person of your word, and have something to show for it. Love is a feeling and if it's not put into action it will appear to be a lie. Always serve the truth to the best of your ability. Intent is internal and true love needs to be lived externally and be shown by God's grace to live on eternally.

Nitpicking

Nobody is perfect, and we are all a work in progress. However, being overly critical is not a sign of love. True love does not focus on imperfections that one cannot change. People who truly love you may not even notice your imperfections or be bothered by them. If someone criticizes your authenticity then they are insulting the core of your character that you shouldn't change. Only a manipulative person hurts someone to

Love of Life

bring them closer to them. The core authenticity of your character should not shift for anyone.

Love bombing

Narcissists tend to love bomb at the beginning of a relationship. They say grandiose things such as "you are perfect" and give excessive compliments. They love to use absolutes consistently: "You are my forever," and, "I'll never hurt you." They deny reality with fantastical thinking. A narcissist will build you up with dreams through words but in reality, devalue you through their actions. Using words consistently such as "never", "forever", and "always" are words manipulators use to ensure certainty in those who live in fear of the future.

"A lying tongue hates its victims, and a flattering mouth works ruins."
(Proverbs 26:28)

Love Language Abuse

Gifts

Prison bail utilized as a reward system

It's the thought that counts behind the gift. Why did they choose the gift they picked for you? Is it a reward for enduring physical abuse? Is it a tracking device? Did they buy you something to silence you for an evil they have done?

Illicit you as property

Is the gift given to you to show off to others and not suitable to your authenticity? Example: jewelry, and clothing. What is the message to others? Are they trying to advertise and project something that is not true to you?

Forcing a new identity

Is it to enforce something they wish you liked? Example: buying a hair dye of a color they know you hate, but they love for you to wear. Buying you an album of their favorite band that they know you do not like to listen to. If you are constantly having to match outfits that is also an indication of loss of identity. Two people should

Love of Life

be strong individually and be extensions of each and not assimilate beyond recognition of individuality.

"Whatever your task, put yourselves into it, as done for the Lord and not for your masters since you know that from the Lord you will receive the inheritance as your reward; you serve the Lord Christ."

(Colossians 3:23)

Love Language Abuse

Acts of Service

Superiority Battle

Draining someone of their humility and self-respect is one of the ultimate crimes against your authentic self. Humility and servitude can easily be abused and viewed as noble. Acts of service are abused when two people are not equally yoked, and one person appears superior to the other. An obligatory act of service absent of love and full of disdain is dishonorable. Contempt and disdain are rarely salvageable traits that the heart may reverse into goodness. They are both damning and can easily become the cause of a divorce.

Emasculating a man or insulting a woman's femininity is a form of abuse. Trying to outdo or underdo each other in nurturing and providing is an abusive cycle that leads to inequality. An imbalance of worthiness will lead to a power struggle that is toxic and abusive. Pride and sloth, the deadly sins are at the battle and it is a losing game no matter who wins. Men and women are different and being equally yoked doesn't mean we have to be the same. Acknowledge each other's differences and compliment them rather than noting them as superior or inferior. Love is about being fair, and keeping it sexy, meaning not abusing each other's biological,

Love of Life

mental, emotional, and physical strengths and weaknesses.

"You, my brothers and sisters, were called to be free. But you do not use your freedom to indulge the flesh; rather serve another humbly in love."

(Galatians 5:13)

Principles

"For God did not give us a spirit of cowardice, but rather a spirit of power and love and of self-discipline."
(2 Timothy 1:7)

Principles are rooted in belief systems. Principles are often governed by pleasure, pain, or peace. If you want peace truth is the way to get there. Pleasure can give you pain, pain can give you pleasure. Release occurs after receiving pain or pleasure. Pleasure can come from good or it can come from bad If the pleasure is from a source of good it will bring peace and growth. If the pleasure comes out of bad it will bring chaos, stagnation, or regression. If the fruit of your decisions has value, then you will have a meaningful life. Peace is in goodness and truth. Pleasure is short-lived and purpose is lived for life.

Success is garnered by how you manage your urges. Discipline is how you show love to yourself and others. To have discipline you must have willpower. You will power by attaining energy. Energy is generated through discipline. Energy is used to heal or hurt, be intentional with your energy. Discipline manages energy. Action is fruitful if it upgrades you rather than distract you from your purpose. Consider bad character a false sense of your highest self, and good character a true sense of your highest self. One can live a lie or live the truth authentically. We must empower ourselves through responsibility, so that we may not be submissive to the powers that are out of our control. We are not to submit and always run from evil, we are to contend and face it.

Being happy is a mood and it does not always have to be sustained if it is counterproductive. If happiness is rooted in a lie let it die. We can be happy with something that isn't right. Happiness comes and goes, but character leaves a lasting impression. It is important to have principles that are unshakeable so that we have a solid foundation to bring us back in check. We must walk in the ways of Jesus Christ - Christian's are not meant to be meek and lukewarm.

"So, because you are lukewarm, and neither hot nor cold, I will spit you out of my mouth."
(Revelations 3:16)

Think of Aslan from The Chronicles of Narnia. Aslan was meant to be a metaphor for Jesus Christ. How does your inner lion or lioness walk? What is your theme song as you prowl this Earth? Here are the laws of prowess:

Lion & Lioness 7 Roars of Conduct

Responsibility

Review

Repent

Release

Renew

Redeem

Rejoice

Love of Life

Lions Creed

When we fall, we are to take full responsibility for ourselves. We are to review what happened in its truest form to prevent repeated behavior. We are to repent for what we have done and what we have failed to do. We must then release any resentment we have toward ourselves and others so that we may not suffer endlessly.

Every movie has a goal. There will be trials and tribulations. We renew our minds in the word of God, and go out and try again to do our best. We redeem ourselves by learning our lessons, protecting ourselves, and others while we contend with evil. We rejoice in our redemption as we move forward, not stifled by past occurrences.

The lion and the lioness are not to be comfortable at all times. They are not to sustain any mood at all times. They are to be challenged, satiate their appetite for life, and rest to have the energy for another day. We are not to indulge in every desire, for a lioness or lion who does, lacks discipline.

Those who lack discipline lack good character, grace, and goodwill. We are not sheep; we are to have prowess. May the powerless who desire good, develop prowess to triumph over evil.

Calling + True Love = Harmony

Love of Life

Happiness comes and goes, but good character with a life well lived is a legend that leaves an imprint on many generations. May our hearts be light as we prowl the path of life the kingdom way.

Mind, Body, Spirit, Soul

"For perverse thoughts separate people from God, and when his power is tested, it exposes the foolish; because wisdom will not enter a deceitful soul, or dwell in a body enslaved to sin. For a holy and disciplined spirit will flee from deceit, and will leave foolish thoughts behind, and will be ashamed at the approach of unrighteousness."
(The Wisdom of Solomon 1:3)

When making decisions you can lead with your mind, body, spirit, or soul. Life is best when all four are in harmony. When it comes to gifts, you lead with their mind - this is why it's the thought that counts. People who lead with their bodies are more likely to be sexual, to really love food, and may have a problem with self-control leading to gluttony and lust. People who lead with their spirit tend to vary in their moods; they are the type to go with what they feel. This could lead to wrath and envy, or kindness and patience. The soul is the authentic self that allows God to recognize you. People who lead with their soul lead with discipline and are being led by divine, or demonic influences. Which do you lead with? Mind, body, spirit, or soul?

What you lead with tends to show how you like to give love, which may not be the same as receiving love. If your giving love language is primarily physical touch, and quality time your potential weaknesses are lust and gluttony, and your strengths are in chastity and temperance. It is useful to be multilingual with love languages and be able to lead with what is necessary for growth.

Look at your love language and assess whether you are virtuous (self-love) or vice ridden (self-hate disguised as love). If your primary love language is quality time, and you spend time overindulging in alcohol, you are not loving yourself. If someone tells you their primary love language and you find that they are leading with vice and not virtue, you cannot trust that they love themselves, and therefore you cannot trust that they can love you.

If someone has an unhealthy form of a virtue, they will make a diabolical match with a person who is dedicated to their vice. If you are too greedy, you may be compatible with someone who is too charitable. If someone has anger problems, they might choose someone who is an overly patient doormat. Even if you are virtuous, there are consequences to overdoing it. It may attract you to a diabolical match due to your dysfunction.

Mind, Body, Spirit, and Soul

The Gift of Love (1 Corinthians 13:1-7)	Vice	Virtue	Love Language
SPIRIT — "If I speak in the tongues of mortals and of angels, but do not have love, I am a noisy gong or a clanging cymbal.	Wrath, Envy	Patience, Kindness	Words of Affirmation
MIND — And if I have prophetic powers, and understand all mysteries and all knowledge, and if I have all faith, so as to remove mountains, but do not have love, I am nothing.	Greed	Charity	Gifts
BODY — If I give away all my possessions, and if I hand over my body so that I may boast, but do not have love, I gain nothing.	Lust, Gluttony	Chastity, Temperance	Physical Touch, Quality Time
SOUL — Love is patient; love is kind; love is not envious or boastful or arrogant or rude. It does not insist on its own way; it is not irritable or resentful; it does not rejoice in wrongdoings, but rejoices in the truth. It bears all things, believes all things, hopes all things, endures all things."	Pride, Sloth	Humility, Diligence	Acts of Service

Love of Life

Mind Wealth

"Let your gentleness be known to everyone. The Lord is near. Do not worry about anything, but in everything by prayer and supplication with thanksgiving let your request be made known to God. And the peace of God, which surpasses all understanding, will guard your hearts and your minds in Christ Jesus."
(Philippians 4:5-7)

Your mind controls possibilities for your life. The spirit is the energy source behind those possibilities, and your body is your processor. The mind is a gateway, which is why knowledge is power. All thoughts start in the mind: hunger, desire, sex. Our composure and exposure dictate the framework from which we think. The ultimate connection one can experience on Earth is when everything is in alignment with the highest authentic self- fulfilling to the (soul), enlightening (mind), peaceful (spirit), and fruitful (body). Set your mind on the virtuous spirit of your soul and your body will be at peace. Fasting is a great way to provide clarity.

If your mind is out of order then your vision is out of whack, and you cannot trust your wants and desires. Since it's the thought that counts behind the gift, you can see how in order or out of order your mindset is at the state of giving a gift. On a primal level, women are more keen to lean to gifts as their receiving love language than a man because men are supposed to be providers. Gifts

is a great way for a man to show how he can provide. How you start a relationship can be reflective of how and why the relationship came to an end. There are always clues.

You should be mindful of how to go about releasing information about yourself. One should show someone who they are before they are taught how to love you. The reason for this is to avoid the possibility of manipulation. After all, before seducing someone wouldn't you want to know who they are before you welcome them into your home? If they don't care to know who you are, then how can they love you?

On a date, a lot of people think about how to impress others and how to get the other person to like them. You should be more interested in discovering the truth of that person's essence, and not be focused on their ability to seduce and convince others to like them. People who focus on other people liking them are insecure. Being alluring is necessary and can be very fun. If you cannot communicate properly through the art of lure, it will be hard to get people interested in who you are.

When discovering someone to fall in love with, one should lead with who they are, what they are doing, how they are doing it, and why they are there, to begin with. If people lead in a different order you must question their motives. If someone states, why they want to love you

Love of Life

before knowing who you are, it is cause for suspicion. If they tell you how they are going to love you before knowing who you are; that is a red flag. If someone leads with what they are doing and shows you nothing about who they are, what are they hiding? What are they missing?

Order matters; it affects how you process everything. When someone approaches your door, your first thought is "who is it?" This is the first thing you should say before allowing anyone into the home of their heart. You do not open the door right away; you look through the peephole. After they announce who they are the next question is, what are you doing here? (What is their intention?) This is followed by how they want to do what they are intend to do, and discovering why they are doing it.

Imagine eating a dish with your eyes closed and only looking at the plate after the meal is finished. You could not process what the food looked like before you ate it all you would know is that you are no longer hungry. When you are full, looking at food is not as appetizing. Before people eat a meal, they sometimes take a picture of it, mesmerized by the perfection and presentation. They can appreciate the nuances of the appearance of different components. If you do not like the appearance, smell or ingredients you may have the knowledge or the sense to reject it. However, if taste is the only sense you

are aware of upon consumption, your judgment may be off.

You should not lead strangers into your bedroom, or report details about what is in your basement to strangers. Imagine if your first question was "How do you want to love me?" and they say, "I want to love you in all the ways you feel loved. What's your love language?" You answer "physical touch" and they respond "Is it okay that I knock on your bedroom window? My love is the bomb, it will blow your mind and your back." The question triggered the body's desire to respond over the mind. If you do not like or respect who they are, then you don't want them having access to your mind, body, spirit, or soul.

After someone passes the door test, the next place is conversation in the living room. You show others how you are living, then then advance to the kitchen or family room. The family room may include other members of your family. The kitchen is where you nourish and cleanse yourself. You bring items from the kitchen to the dining table. Only a familiar person may enter the kitchen at their own will with your permission. You must build trust before entering the kitchen. Afterall, your kitchen has food, and if someone raids your kitchen, and has your knives, you will be at risk. A guest may want to replace your food, increase your food, or poison it.

Love of Life

The basement is where you share your memories, and the stuff you may or may not need in the future. Some relationships reach the bedroom and never the basement. Some people have a bed in their basement, and never allow you into their room. It is all about intimacy and comfort levels. Question the individual who has you crawl through their bedroom window, or hides in the basement. They don't fully trust you, and it's likely because they have dark secrets. People who say they are looking for someone to do things for them absent from caring for who the person is wants a slave. A person who wants someone they can serve absent of the character wants a master. It is very important that the first line of questioning starts with "who are you?" rather than "what can you do for me?" when it comes to building any type of relationship.

If someone doesn't care who you are then how can you mean anything to them? What you did may have meaning but if they don't care who the source is then your authentic soul is irrelevant to the gift they received from you. Just because someone appreciates what you gave them, doesn't mean they appreciate you as an individual.

7 Questions before falling in love

Who are they?

What are they doing?

Mind, Body, Spirit, and Soul

How are they doing it?

Why are they doing it?

Where are they going?

When do they want to come to me?

How much is it going to cost me?

Until someone is solidified in their identity, you cannot trust their wants or their wishes. Beware of cost - not all investments have positive returns. If you let someone live in your house and they haven't signed the lease, they are not liable to you. They can go whenever they please, and a verbal promise isn't enough to keep them accountable. Until you are married to another, any promise can be made void. You should not make promises without full commitment and follow through. You should not expect wife/husband behavior or benefits unless under the guise of marriage. The Bible does not discuss boyfriend/girlfriend relationships. The purpose of dating is to see whom you'd like to marry and possibly start a family with in the future.

Love once overdosed makes one sick, in fact one may not call it love at that point – for it has turned into obsession. One cannot treasure something that they cannot lose or admire. If you were getting something free for a long time, you may resent paying for it. It doesn't matter how valuable someone is; what matters is your

Love of Life

experience with them. If you feel they are what you ultimately want, and you are ready for them, then investment will seem like an indisputable choice. How you process your experience highly depends on the order and amount of access.

There is nothing like sustaining a great loss and having nothing to show for it due to a grand investment and the lack of a contract. It's embarrassing and the cost is devastating. Imagine the house is your heart and someone destroys the walls and carpets with no contract or damage deposit. The person paying the bill will be you and the guest will not be liable for anything.

As you assess the damage you will wonder why you let them get that far in the first place. Imagine having to explain the damage to someone you actually want to reside in your heart for life? Their title was "guest" (boyfriend/girlfriend) and yet they slept over every day, stole your food, took your favorite pot, changed the faucets to their liking, and changed the flooring to dirt. Access to your home should be limited and it is in your best interest. When moving in with someone you don't want to constantly be reminded of the former tenant's presence when they were not a partner but a temp.

Not all guests can spend the night, enter the kitchen, enter the basement, or come into your bedroom at their will. It's all about investment, and access should only be granted with concrete agreements on titles. People can say all they want and have nobody hold them accountable in court. This is not to say that no one can violate a marriage, but the contract will require them to honor the promises they made to the person they married. It is not just a piece of paper; it is a vow before God.

     Marriage represents stability. Getting married is a process; there is the engagement period, premarital counseling. There are stages before the wedding. During the wedding, there are witnesses that make you feel accountable for the promises made before God. Some people get lucky and still end up with the right person after doing things out of order. Even then, it wouldn't have harmed them by doing things in the order God ordains. Aligning with God's will and way blesses your relationship.

"The fear of the Lord is the beginning of wisdom, and the knowledge of the Holy One is insight."
(Proverbs 9:10)

Love of Life

Body Wealth

"Let us live honorably as in the day, not in reveling and drunkenness, not in debauchery and licentiousness, not in quarreling and jealousy. Instead put on the Lord Jesus Christ, and make no provision for the flesh, to gratify its desires."
(Romans 13:13-14)

The body has its own memory system and it does not lie, and it also has a hard time forgetting more so than your mind does. It can be activated by something perceived, imagined, or experienced. Body language is the first language you learn, and is the most universally transmitted language. It showcases more truth than our words, for it is more unconscious than conscious. The unconscious mind does not have a filter the way the conscious mind does.

Quality time is associated with the body because it requires temperance, undivided attention, and presence. In a sense you just need somebody to be there for you. If they are not there in body, it is hard to determine if they are in spirit, soul, or mind. On a primal level, men want to spread their seed which is why physical touch is a love language they are more keen to have as their primary love language. Often at times, you will see a woman with a great body with a man who has a lot of money to provide because on a primal level they are compatible with their primal needs. Although, they may gain resentment for each other if their spirit and soul are ignored or incompatible. Often at times, people feel disrespected if they are only used for their money or their body. This may foster the other love languages negatively creating wrath (words of affirmation) and pride (acts of service). You can lead with your mind, body, spirit, or soul. It is all up to you. If you lead with the body, it will be hard to find discernment of your life's purpose. Your song will likely be out of alignment with the harmony God had in store for following Him.

Your body can be turned on by a variety of different elements. You can be turned on by watching pornography, or a physical encounter. You can orgasm while being raped. Just because you receive a release doesn't mean it is a good thing. People wonder if sex will be bad if they wait until marriage. If you are truly in love in a marriage then making love won't be a bad thing or a destroyer of the relationship. Sex starts in the mind, not in the body. Sex is not meant for us to use to discover "if" you could love the person because your body cannot discern that simply from sex. If your spirit does not connect with your physical bond, and you create a soul tie you will create chaos in your life. If you and your partner wait until marriage, you significantly reduce your chances of contracting a sexually transmitted disease. It's also best for the children you may create.

Love of Life

Your body can "Get Off", and your body can "Get On." People who "Get Off" live in their heads. People who "Get On" live with their mind, body, spirit, and soul connected. Getting Off entails using your imagination without someone else's participation, or it can be a natural organic response to something physical. When one Gets Off on imagination, they are not connected or humanizing the people involved. This is why masturbation and pornography are harmful. It's not healthy to dissect people into body parts, making their wellbeing, mind, spirit, and soul is irrelevant. Fantasizing about doing things to people who may not want things done to them is unhealthy.

When you live in your head too much, enjoying reality can become virtually impossible. If we have to narrate the fantasies in our heads with precision, it will likely not come naturally to our partner and if it doesn't come naturally and is not enjoyable; it will create a disconnect. You are simply bonding yourself to an addiction to fantasy with a person as your object when you Get Off. It gives someone a high and the hangover is empty and unfulfilling. Getting Off triggers dopamine, and Getting On triggers dopamine. Dopamine sends signals to your brain that a reward is not the way. Getting On has rewards, getting off has consequences. The consequence may be lack of fulfillment or a prize that causes destruction.

Mind, Body, Spirit, and Soul

Dopamine is neither good or bad but it reflects desire. It is the arrow in your way of thinking and the target is either a virtue or vice. Vice separates you from purpose. Addicts live in a reality where their desire overrides their sense of discipline. They fall out of order, lose control, and are drawn to a master that serves destruction.

Fantasy can be a good creative tool for development and escape. Imagination can be visionary to help one align with what they may be divinely assigned to do. However, if fantasy is lived in as a home and not a vacation or break one must ask themselves, where are the works? One must assess why reality lost its base in living life. When fantasy matches reality there is no longer a bridge in between; it is simply just reality.

Getting On requires connection and does not have this same result; it is fruitful in its release and pleasurable to both sides as a result. Sex should be explored in the context of marriage so you can please one another mutually and learn and grow together. If you do too much on your own it will be hard to connect. If you have sex with too many people you will have too many comparisons and that will distract you from connection. Two people can bond in Getting Off and this is not to be confused with Getting On which has a connection. Without sober judgment fulfillment is an illusion. It is the difference between making love and having sex. Two are

Love of Life

to become one - if the oneness does not involve two people in mental, spiritual, emotional, and physical union then it is just sex and not making love. One is not making love when one is dishonoring God. Delayed gratification is more fulfilling then instant gratification. Delaying sex has gratification that instant sex will not fulfill in the long run.

Many people think having oral sex or anal sex is a substitute for not having sex before marriage. It defeats the purpose of waiting, which is not only about not having a child until it's time. If a prize is to be able to eat a lollipop and someone goes and licks it and puts it back in the wrapper and says they didn't eat it - it's a half-truth. Some may even say it is worse to have a taste of what you want rather than fully consuming it. Your soul will have a tie, and marriage happens when you tie the knot. You do not want multiple ties before you tie the knot. It is best not to be naughty. It's not wise to allow your body and soul to make contracts that your mind and spirit have not made. Even if the other person has decided to spend the rest of the life with you until you two have made a vow before God it doesn't count. Waiting until marriage is one of the hardest things for someone to accomplish when they love someone. If you can gain discipline in this area you may be able to do and conquer a lot in your life.

There is power in delayed gratification; it helps one thrive instead of survive. If your reward makes you feel like you "survived" then you likely do not need it. If it makes you thrive, then it is what you need. Delayed gratification helps "Getting On" to reach capacity and longevity. In following discipline through sex, you learn to honor the person you are with. It builds a bond that instant gratification cannot create. When you are in love with someone, and you make love to them, their imperfections won't be as much in the way of the pleasure you experience with one another. Order matters because it affects processing. Those who complain about processing and are living their life out of order are not good examples to listen to in terms of advice. Make no comparison, for it won't be fair or accurate.

Don't make assumptions. Sometimes the fantasy is your own and you have to check in with the person you are dating to see if they are dreaming the same dream. Sometimes people are not dreaming the same dream, but are simply dedicated to the same illusion. Trauma often creates a new dream, and it often isn't a better one. Clarity of God creates a new dream, and it is the one that is right for you.

Oxytocin is a neural transmitter and a hormone that bonds people. It bonds a mother to a child, and it bonds a man and a woman. Oxytocin bonding is formed through cuddling, hugging, kissing, having sex, and listening to music together. The hormone resets a woman's emotions, and if she isn't oxytocin bonding with

her partner, the more neurotic she is likely to become. Oxytocin bonding creates excitement, trust, and it can overwrite past behaviors and neurological programming. A woman's body will naturally do this regardless of whether or not she says she won't get emotionally attached to a man. Your body has its own memory system and it will condition itself based on what it is exposed to. Before a man and a woman have sex with someone it is crucial to understand this. You cannot override subconscious bonding for it is out of your control.

Marriage is an example of a calling that includes mind, body, spirit, and soul. It's best to be with someone who you know would be a good mother or father to a child. Your marriage should complement and serve your life's purpose. If it does not enlighten you or give you peace it's not likely to be ordained by God.

The basis of marriage should follow serving your life's purpose with a spiritual connection before your body makes a bond. It is hard to have discernment once the body has oxytocin bonded with an intimate partner. When people are connected at heart and spirit their chest will turn towards the other person, and when it is their mind their heads tilt in. When two people are sexually connected you can see it in pictures. Their hips will often touch one another.

Mind, Body, Spirit, and Soul

Intimacy is shown through quality time and physical touch all of which affect the body. Who you decide to share your body with exposes your intentions and speaks volumes about your principles. If your love languages are quality time/physical touch you may have a rough time waiting until marriage to have sex. Food and sex are natural drivers that are very hard to discipline. That's what makes addiction in these areas so difficult. One can abstain from sex, but one can only abstain from food for so long. Fasting gives you clarity. You may not feel loved by who you are with during the course of the relationship if you are not timely with your body. It is highly encouraged to learn to appreciate the other languages until you are married. Just because something is your primary love language doesn't mean you cannot learn to appreciate the other languages. Something unfortunate can happen to your body and the other love languages may be your only choice. If all you have is love is only reflected in the body then your love will be in vain and conditional.

Those whose favorite love language is physical touch, usually struggle the most to find true love. This is because they have to suppress the language that they understand the best to navigate true love. They have to lead and help through another love language that they may not primally desire. For instance, let's say your favorite part of work is getting paid. Getting paid is like getting laid in terms of physical touch as a love language.

Love of Life

Who has a better life? The person who loves the money but hates their job, or the person that loves their job that may or may not be paid a lot of money?

    If a man goes to a dealership and says "Can I take the car without contract?" and the woman says "yes", The man will likely use that car anyhow because there is nothing to hold him accountable. The actual value of the car is irrelevant, what is relevant is what you are allowed to do with it. People look at value based on experience and not necessarily price.

    If a luxury car allows anyone to have and drive it, people will question if it is truly a luxury. If you question yourself others will question you. A lot of people will think things are okay in this life as long as two people "agree". No accountability leaves no responsibility, which leads to recklessness without empathetic connect. It's the difference between stealing an item vs buying one. The thrill of stealing vs buying is different. The thief and the buyer may use the same vehicle and go the distance. The process of ownership changes the relationship.

    If the process is done orderly, one may appreciate what they have acquired differently. You can walk on foot in your life but a car will get you places further in due time. A lot of people will refer to sex as testing the car before you buy it. When one test drives a car, they are not allowed to go get takeout food and accidentally spill

Mind, Body, Spirit, and Soul

milkshake in the vehicle. The test driver has parameters and rules. You will not be allowed to freely get milk. Don't lead with dishonor or fall prey to fallacies spawned from an irresponsible mentality. Whether you get the car for free or pay with money and time, both modes ended up with the car off the lot, but the person will process the value and importance of the vehicle differently due to processing and not the actual value of the vehicle.

Love of Life

Spirit Wealth

"Finally, be strong in the Lord and in the strength of his power. Put on the whole armor of God, so that you may be able to stand against the wiles of the devil. For our struggle is not against enemies of blood and flesh, but against the rulers, against the authorities, against the cosmic powers of this present darkness, against the spiritual forces of evil in the heavenly places. Therefore take up the whole armor of God, so that you may be able to withstand on that evil day, and having done everything, to stand firm. Stand therefore, and fasten the belt of truth around your waist, and put on the breastplate of righteousness."
(Ephesians 6:10-14)

Spiritual wealth is influenced by good and bad spirits. There are seven gifts of the Holy Spirit. Wisdom, knowledge, counsel, fortitude, understanding, piety, and fear of the Lord. If a spirit does not give you any of these gifts, it's not from the Holy Spirit. If it is not the Holy Spirit it is not to be trusted. Your spirit is tied to your emotions. When you hear someone say "I felt the holy spirit" they are in tune with a feeling. You do not want to be devoid of the Holy Spirit. There are all kinds of spirits and they go after anyone and everyone. It is highly valuable to be emotionally and spiritually wealthy. It is an energy source that will fill you up, and aid you in following through with your actions. Through being wealthy, you can give to others.

Everyone has an energy bar and when two become one the energy bar should expand. Lifeline love is when your energy bar is connected to their lack of energy which naturally depletes your original source of energy. Expansion pack love adds to your bars and exceeds what you knew was possible. Your energy bars bond with one another and you can feel each other's emotions.

Bonds

Bonds are created over time, and if strong can be recognized as a possibility immediately. A bond can be created via the body, spirit, or the mind, and can die. We end up bonding with different people who are in our likeness. We bond over things like music, shared experiences, or having similar thoughts, and feelings. Not all bonds are bad, and not all bonds are good. Good bonds help you grow and illuminate in life. Bad bonds destroy you and leave you in a dark place.

Trauma bonds stem from dark places, and once the drugs of the effect of that relationship wear off, and you sober up, you can gain clarity on the bonds built. If your hurt is what binds you two together, you have a trauma bond. Trauma bonds cause further damage through repeated learned behavior with abuse to create

Love of Life

attachment. They build you up and break you down. Bonds can cause bondage. Toxic bonds have the symptoms of a drug addict in withdrawal or can produce anxiety on sight. The toxicity creates a feeling of not being able to live with or without. It makes you hyper-focus in a destructive way. It is an itch that makes you scratch until the skin of your identity comes off. Some people fear individuality, especially if they do not want to face their demons, which makes them prime and ready for unhealthy attachments.

Narcissists are energy vampires. They create hypnotic bonds. A person may say, "I know this person is bad, I just can't help myself." It has drug-like effects; lack of control, lots of imagination, and draining hangovers. You will not be yourself; you will be a skeleton yourself. The cause of death will be anxiety, concern for control, uncontrolled anger, dependence instead of interdependence, bitterness, envy, and selfishness.

You can tell how much someone has bonded with you by the way they speak to you and of you. If someone says "the wife" "the kids" "the friend I told you about" it may be a minor indication that they are not close to you, or may have a bit of disdain for you. "My" is far more personal and caring, when someone says "my kids" it indicates closeness. You know the person is beginning to have contempt for you if they switch from "my" to "the".

Spiritual Warfare

If you feel you have bad spirits haunting you or around you, you must close the gateway that gave them access. Whether that's the Ouija board, music, movies, horoscopes, tarot cards, drugs, yoga (yoga is a Hindu practice, not just a stretching exercise), or anything that may be occult in practice you must seize it immediately.

Symptoms of spiritual warfare include anxiety, restlessness, unexplained illness, nightmares, sleep paralysis, unexplained sensations, and being out of character with your identity. Anything that tortures you that is out of your control is demonic. Cut off all gateways. Call out the spirit by name if you encounter it, and rebuke it in the name of Jesus. It may sound silly but there are plenty of true stories written where using Jesus name works.

Love of Life

Soul Wealth

Your soul is rooted in your calling; it entails your authenticity laced with your discipline.

Your soul is associated with your calling that God has called you to serve. It is your authentic self aligned with your life's purpose. It is core to our souls that we learn discipline, and in that discipline, we learn order. The soul is governed by honor, and respect which is why it is attached to Acts of service. The soul is at the top of the hierarchy and should be the highest-ranked out of the components to serve God. Your soul wealth will be based on your purpose. You must discover your purpose before they are able to fulfill it. God gives us gifts, and we are to honor them as we go about our path in life. Look at your gifts and see how you can grow and maintain them for the good of yourself and others. Have conversations with the Lord, and he will guide you on what to do.

Bonds vs Connections

You must discern the difference between a bond and a connection. The difference is not in strength but in its properties. Connections never die and can only be recognized and not created. It is divine, true, effortless, timeless, and not man-made through manipulation or obsession. It is rooted in the authenticity of your soul and is the best vein to make unconditional love possible. It is

Mind, Body, Spirit, and Soul

a soul tie that lives on forever. You can bond with whom you are connected, but the connection itself cannot be controlled; it is simply ordained. God is at the center of true connection. Connections are rare, and most people only have a few their lifetime. True love is in connection and is unconditional. It is spiritual and aligns with the goodness and authenticity of your soul. When entering a marital relationship, it is important to have these discernments. It is in our best interest that we know God, and have a relationship to properly recognize connections that lead to our ultimate fulfillment.

Soul Ties

A soul tie will always have you feeling that you must be together or return to one another. Sometimes people misinterpret their despair as a sign they are meant to be with the person. Soul ties are like dopamine triggers. There are some people we may desire endlessly until we understand the craving and heal ourselves to the truth. You can have a soul tie with someone who was bad for you as sugar is to teeth. You can have someone who may appear good for you as a healthy food. However, a food may not sit well in your stomach and therefore derail the purpose of eating and satisfying your needs.

Whether someone is good for you or bad for you it doesn't erases the good memories and fun that you may have had with them. People remember how you

Love of Life

made them feel and people often return to their soul ties to regenerate their feeling. Some people pick partners based on their pain. For example, a person who fears abandonment may pick someone who over emphasizes that they will never leave. Separation hurts and people try to heal their pain by reattachment. When it comes to what hurt you sometimes the best way out is through the pain. Detox doesn't mean you need to return to the drug it just shows you how toxic the drug really was. It is best to understand that good feelings may not always equal good for your purpose.

Narcissism

"There are six things that the LORD hates, seven that are an abomination to him: haughty eyes, a lying tongue, hands that shed innocent blood, a heart that devises wicked plans, feet that hurry to run to evil, a lying witness who testifies falsely, and one who sows discord in a family."
(Proverbs 6:16-19)

Pride and lack of empathy are the roots of narcissism. Narcissists are created through neglect or overindulgence. You cannot be diagnosed with Narcissism until adolescence. Clinically, professionals look for five or more traits listed in the diagnostic manual to diagnose people. Narcissists are childlike about satisfying their desires; they have no concept of satisfying needs that don't aid their own. Emotionally they are quite immature.

Narcissism is not selective, just as mental retardation is not selective in terms of its output. A true narcissist has their toxic behaviors reflected in all their relationships, and some have it worse than others. Narcissists are self-centered, demanding, needy, entitled, easily angered, unforgiving, and difficult to be around. Pride is what created the fallen angel the devil, it was how the serpent was able to seduce Adam and Eve. The devil wanted to be above God. .

Love of Life

> "You said in your heart, "I will ascend to heaven; I will raise my throne above the stars of God; I will sit on the mount of assembly on the heights of Zaphon; I will ascend to the tops of the clouds, I will make myself like the Most High."
> (Isaiah 14:12)

When seducing Eve, the serpent appealed to Eve's desire to seek the truth.

> "But the serpent said to the woman, "You will not die; for God knows that when you eat of it your eyes will be opened, and you will be like God, knowing good and evil."
> (Genesis 3:4)

Her curiosity and desire to be like God led to her temptation of the fruit. Wanting to be your own God, creates an illusion that if you create your own rules, and justify all desires, you will be happy and fulfilled. We are not to set the rules; we are to listen and obey God. Satan seduced her with half-truths, and her desire got the best of her.

> "Then the eyes of both were opened and they knew they were naked; and they sewed fig leaves together and made loincloths for themselves."
> (Genesis 3:7)

Pride takes no responsibility unless it garners profit. When God confronted Adam and Eve about covering themselves, they took no responsibility for eating the forbidden fruit. Adam blamed Eve, and Eve blamed the serpent. Do not be like the serpent be a lion and take responsibility.

Results of Narcissism

"Your eyes will see strange things, and your mind utter perverse things."
(Proverbs 23:33)

Narcissists are about image, and they want to appear to be winning all the time even if they are losing. You do not want to play games with a narcissist. You will always lose, for their rules are not grounded in reality. They will use cheat codes and put on invincibility mode at times when they are supposed to face repercussions. They may be blasphemous about God's work and say things such as "God did this" about things that were done of their own freewill. For example, they may stalk someone and pretend to run into them and call it "divine intervention". They may refer to something as God's plan when it was a manipulative plot created by their demonic ways.

Hoovering is a technique narcissist use to keep people under their rule. When you break up with them, they may pretend the relationship isn't over. They may make plans that would be too embarrassing to cancel so that you feel forced to show up. They will abuse holidays as a way to get to you. They will utilize your friends and family to send messages they shouldn't send that make you feel

Love of Life

forced to communicate with them. They will starve the securities you have (contact with family and friends, access to finances, etc.), and feed your insecurities (low self-esteem, fear, shame, etc.). They will feed your fantasies and your nightmares without grounds in reality.

The Unicorn & The Pegasus

Lions and lionesses are real animals. They exist and they are on the prowl as we speak. Narcissists are like unicorns, they exist as much as they do not exist. Unicorns look like real horses except they have a horn. Narcissists like unicorns are mythical, except the horseplay is real and can do some real damage. Narcissists are mythical in terms of their thinking and processing.

People who fall prey to the narcissist's spell are like Pegasus. Pegasus are under the mythical dream created by the unicorn. The unicorn is at the "advantage" because they created the dream, the Pegasus just has to operate around it. The unicorns are the fantasy makers, Pegasus's are the fantasy lovers. If you know more about fictional creatures and fictional people than you do real people - chances are - you are going to be more susceptible to being a unicorn or a pegasus. Both want to escape the horribleness of reality and know more about fiction then how real life operates.

Narcissism

Nobody wants to kill the dream that makes them feel good. It's like a song where you love the melody but the lyrics are evil. Many people will say when confronted "don't ruin it for me" or "don't ruin the magic." They are looking to feel good rather than do the right thing. Reality is too hard for them to deal with so they choose to escape. It kills the soul, because your soul is rooted in your calling, and your calling is your dream, and if you do not perceive or have faith in a better dream, reality will be utterly devastating.

Pleasure is the foundation of fantasy; calling is the foundation of a dream. Unicorn and pegasus are pleasure seekers; lion and lioness follow their calling. Unicorn and pegasus are living lies, lion and lionesses are living truth. Both the unicorn and the pegasus are admired, and they are both magical in their own right. The unicorn has beauty despite its horn, and the pegasus has beauty in its wings and grace. Since the Pegasus has wings, it thinks it can save the unicorn; however, it often gets poked by the unicorn's horn, inflicting pain. That pain is not just prickly, it has a venomous sting of a jellyfish.

A unicorn's aura has a particular light, just like how jellyfish may have a light inside them. They can hypnotize you with their glow, but can paralyze you with their poison, messing with brain and heart, and leave you feeling with a terrible feeling in the pit of your stomach. Some jellyfish are pretty dangerous, and unicorns are pretty and dangerous.

The pegasus flies high, and when it tries to get grounded in reality the unicorn stabs them and makes them doubt that their feet are supposed to touch the ground. The unicorn needs the Pegasus to believe that it is supposed to stay in the sky so that the unicorn has grounds to do as they please. The unicorn will keep you away from the grounds you are supposed to walk with God on. When you try to get grounded in reality, they will make you doubt yourself. This is not to say that the pegasus does not deny reality as well. They believe in the dream created by the unicorn and want it to be real so badly. Maintenance of illusions is nobody's cure, it's part of the disease.

Pegasus are typically good people who have fallen for the wrong things. They believe in fantasy and are naïve about the repercussions. A unicorn can be attracted to another unicorn as well. Some high-level narcissists end up with lower-level narcissists as their slaves. Like an apprentice learning the ropes of being a master.

Just because you are suffering abuse, doesn't mean you aren't capable of being an abuser as well. The difference between the unicorn and the Pegasus is that the Pegasus can flee the false reality that the unicorn created and eventually find true love. The unicorn knows no other dream than that under spells of the unwell, and as long as

they are unwell their love will never be true. Many believe that two people in love are dreaming the same dream, and for some people, that dream is a false prophecy. All it takes is one disingenuous character to ruin the premise.

Can the unicorn be cured? The power of God is limitless, and the unicorn would have to surrender its pride and remove their horn. Most unicorns feel they would die without their horn which is why you will likely not see them cured. They'd have to die in their own beliefs and submit to the savior Jesus Christ, a narcissist cured is a miracle. They would have to surrender their pride and have a healthy form of humility, and connect with others empathetically.

The Pegasus needs a cure as well. Both the unicorn and the pegasus need to learn how to face reality. The pegasus will have to create healthy boundaries, learn how to develop a healthy form of humility, and not make other people their God. Both the unicorn and the pegasus would have to surrender their fantastical beliefs and get rooted in the truth. Their works in their life must have a true target, and their arrow must point in a virtuous way. Faith without works is dead. Works without faith is an aimless dream. Narcissists create problems or take advantage of a problem. Here are seven traits and signs to spot narcissism:

Love of Life

7 Signs you are under narcissistic abuse

- They make you doubt reality
- Your sense of security is rooted in their behavior
- You feel a loss of identity, and yet are consumed by seeking their love and validation
- You are ashamed of what you have done, and what you failed to do due to their influence
- They nurture low self-esteem and destroy the things you once loved about yourself
- They have all your energy. It doesn't matter if it is positive or negative, just as long as it is theirs.
- You live life in fear, instead of love for life

Narcissism

7 Signs you may be dealing with a Narcissist

- They have contempt for you
- They compulsively lie
- When trying to resolve an issue they manipulate and or threaten you
- They encourage you to acquire their addictive traits
- They feed your insecurity through scrutiny and fill your security with love bombing
- They are self-centered and cannot think of you outside themselves.
- They devalue you and put you in a state of confusion while supporting illusions that will never be a reality

Love of Life

7 Bad traits that make you suspectable Narcissistic Abuse

- Low self-esteem
- Trouble setting boundaries
- Naivety and overly trusting others
- You act on what you feel absent of truth and faith in God
- Lack of identity
- You worship people as if they are God
- Resistance to learning a lesson, and condemning yourself

Narcissism

7 Good traits that attract Narcissist

- Authentically empathetic and love unconditionally
- Heroic and doesn't give up
- Positive
- Forgiving
- Generous
- Talented
- Strong-willed

Love of Life

It is crucial to preserve the good traits that attracted the narcissist in your life to you. It is also crucial to heal your bad traits so that you kill your attraction to them. The number one trait a narcissist looks for is naivety. Being naïve will allow someone possible access to all your good traits. All predators search for this trait, they look for someone who doesn't have a good security system or a wide-open door. People pleasers do not have doors, and narcissists walk right in, create a door and password and block others out. Narcissists seek people who are not likely to fight back. A naïve person with low self-esteem is the easiest target for a narcissist. Not every person with low self-esteem is naïve, and not everyone who is naïve has low self-esteem.

Having healthy self-esteem and awareness will help guard one against narcissistic abuse. A person who has attractive traits the narcissist wants, will not be susceptible to their abuse if they are aware of the abuse and have the strength and willpower to reject it due to their healthy self-esteem. It is crucial to hold on to the good traits despite the narcissist's attraction to them. If you change the good traits you will be susceptible to becoming like them. You do not want to kill these traits; you want to heal what made you susceptible to falling under the spell of the narcissist.

The narcissist sees the darkness as familiar. They are familiar with artificial light that glows in the dark, and the sunlight is blinding. The night light they have is not artificial to them; in fact, they may think it's even better than sunlight. Just like artificial light they can turn their good and bad traits on and off when it benefits them. They will see the fake plants they have in their room under artificial light as beautiful and everlasting. The narcissist doesn't feel what you are feeling when you describe the warmth of the sun. When you enter into the sunlight after being in the dark for so long you naturally wince. After adjustments you are able to accept and indulge in the light, but not everyone reaches the adjustment period. Some people have light sensitivity that developed due to the darkness in their life.

    Imagine describing light to someone who has hardly seen daylight. They have been in the basement their whole life, and the night light is all that is familiar. Artificial light may have some warmth, but it will never compare to the capacity of the warmth of the sun. You can describe how the sunlight actually helps things grow, melts the ice, and nurtures all living things. However, they will not have the capacity to understand because their baseline is artificial light. You still need water to live; however, artificial plants do not need water. The water can be used for decoration, but it will never seep in, and create growth. The plant will remain the same and frozen in time, like the narcissist who remains immaturely at whatever stage they were traumatized at. Both artificial light and sunlight can discuss the creation of rainbows but the meaning and reasoning will not be the same.

Love of Life

Some people are good at imitation - they can create a fake rose and spray it with water and say it is exactly like the rose in the garden with raindrops. They may even say it's better because it doesn't change and stays at the stage it was created. The sunlight is God's light, and the artificial light is mankind's illusion of it. We can see the artificial light and touch it, God's light we can see and feel it and be in touch with it if we desire a relationship with Him. Some people hide in the shade, some people hide in the basement. When people truly fall in love, they see God's light in each other with a reflected peace and understanding of grace.

Narcissists are emotionally immature and are like a child in the basement. Narcissism is a personality disorder, and personalities are formed at a young age. Once they are an adult it is too late, their learning capacity reaches its limits in possibilities for expansion. At that point, a love that expands you (otherwise known as expansion pack love) is not available. Only someone who can take love out of you (otherwise known as lifeline pack love) are possible means of togetherness. Narcissist are charming and know how to tempt people. Serpents are everywhere but solitude is not the solution.

The trick is to have healthy boundaries and to surround your vulnerability with a healthy form of discernment. The tactic is to have vulnerability with a cadence of sensibility grounded in reality plus a strength

Narcissism

to recover from hurt. The strength is not in the wall; the strength is in conquering overall. What makes someone susceptible to abuse is not a weakness. It is vulnerability in combination with a lack of discernment. It is that combination that gets someone brainwashed and abused.

If you were able to discern something was bad and you were still vulnerable then your boundaries need better protection, if you were not able to discern and you were hurt, then it is your discernment that needs clarity. Choose to grow in protection, choose grace with vulnerability. Good discernment with vulnerability makes an incredibly powerful, admirable, human being.

There are four ways people deal with a narcissist: they try to be heroic and save them, give them positive reinforcement, negative reinforcement, or become a neutralizer. The positive and negative reinforcer gives energy to the narcissist, and you do NOT want to give them more energy. Energy is the supply for the gas tank that leads them to their own reckoning. The courageous hero tries to save them but gets hurt the more they try. There is no way to win on an unfair playing field. It's like playing a video game against a final boss that is programmed to never die but to take energy bars away from you. It's best to avoid interacting with them completely.

The neutralizer doesn't get hurt; they understand what they are dealing with, and do not participate in the reckoning. They do not incite conversations that elicit "to

Love of Life

be continued;" they give flat answers with flat energy or divert the conversation to a new topic. The best way to deal with a narcissist is to bore them and divert attention away from their negativity. For example:

Narcissism

Unicorn

I wonder if Becky's hair is falling out or whether it was pulled out last night.

Pegasus
...(Long silence)

Unicorn looks puzzled at Pegasus.

Unicorn
Do you remember when Becky's hair was good?

Pegasus
Hmmm.

Unicorn
Have you seen Becky lately?

Pegasus
No. (This is not a lie. Always tell the truth.)

Unicorn

Oh my gosh, let's stalk her Instagram story, open up your phone.

Pegasus

You just reminded me that I need to charge my phone. I actually gotta go and I need the battery life for GPS home. (Don't let anyone drain the battery that you need to go in the right direction in life).

Love of Life

For empathetic people, the above method may feel weird and bad. However, the narcissist will do the same to you but in a destructive way. Let's say you order a box of donuts and there is always one pink donut in the mix. You can state that there is a pink donut and the narcissist will challenge your reality and say there isn't one. You can literally open up the box and show them and say "See, there is the pink donut." They may look at you and say, "Your shirt is dirty. You should change it. Do you even do laundry? (mumbles) I guess paying attention to those donuts is getting to you. Your shirt doesn't even fit you the same way." The love language of acts of service (sloth), mixed with quality time (gluttony) is now turned into hate language. They have attacked your soul and your body. They will hit you where it hurts, and it may hurt so much that you may forget the original source of the conversation.

You cannot win an argument with someone who doesn't operate from truth, if you believe a liar you will be lost. Liars are lost even when they believe they are found. Liars believe that belief can conquer truth. Sometimes narcissists will go silent and look away from you with their head held high. When you neutralize them, you are in a sense mirroring the truth in contrast to their behavior without energy. You are telling the truth, and you are not creating more negativity or drama. You state facts, and refrain from offering opinions or emotional reactions, and

bore them away from you. The best thing to do is leave if you can, but if you have a narcissist you cannot fully escape either due to blood relation or work, be mindful. Don't take anything personally, and do not engage in an empathetic way at your own detriment.

"No one, when tempted, should say, "I am being tempted by God"; for God cannot be tempted by evil and he himself tempts no one. But one is tempted by your own desire, being lured and enticed by it then when that desire has conceived, it gives birth to sin, and that sin, when it is fully grown, gives birth to death."
(James 1:13-15)

Note how the serpent told Adam and Eve their eyes would be open once they ate the fruit. He was telling them that God, who was supposed to be their light was blinding them. This made Eve skeptical, and being skeptical does not qualify intelligence. The narcissist is comfortable in the dark and not everyone sees their behavior in the light. The devil often disguises themselves as an angel of light. He makes you curious and skeptical about things that are outside of the truth and outside of goodness. They know what to hide, and what to provide to seduce the world. They love naïve people, who love unconditionally, for they are an energy source of light that just keeps on giving, a Santa Claus that gives to them whether they are naughty or nice. The stronger the person is, the better source of supply they will be for the narcissist. Not everyone under the narcissist's spell is weak; some are just open and vulnerable.

Love of Life

Vulnerability in itself is not negative but it can be used negatively based on purpose. Narcissists desire vulnerable people or people just as wicked as they are. Some narcissists love challenges and will find a strong person and try to make them as vulnerable or as wicked as possible. As long as there is an opening you can be susceptible to narcissistic abuse.

Narcissist go through cycles like seasons, a season of pretending to be the light of the vulnerable person they have consumed and living their darkness with those who are alike. Their actions are based on how they want to look to the world (pride), and how they feel inside (wrath, lust, greed, envy, gluttony, sloth).

Cerebral Narcissist

A cerebral narcissist values their intelligence and cares about righteousness. They are critical of people's intelligence and have a superiority complex. They are diplomatic and love to create dependence from their audience. They operate like the government. They govern how things run in the relationship. Money and status will be huge motivators for them. They may steal money from people or use money to manipulate people to do things for them. The love language, Gifts, is likely to be a primary love language for a cerebral narcissist to show "love". They may give to charity openly to receive clout, or they may be stingy in a greedy way to protect their assets. They can be

a con artist as well who takes money from vulnerable wealthy people. They may encourage their romantic partner not to work to secure their partners dependence by cutting off their means of independence.

What appears to be a kind gesture from a cerebral narcissist usually has an ulterior motive. Their actions are more mental than emotional. They are known to be quite cold which usually makes them quite hard to bond with sexually and emotionally. They love jobs that are rooted in authority or mechanical creations. They dissect people by picking them apart and objectifying them. They may even reverse engineer their victim's goals by utilizing reverse psychology. They have a way to cut people with their words and do not tend to handle criticism very well. They are often admired due to their ability to acquire wealth or their incredible charm or whit. They will be sure to advertise their donations to acquire fans and increase nobility. They demand honor and respect while faking humility with a sense of pride.

Somatic Narcissist

A somatic narcissist fixates on the body. They take pride in the body. They are particular with how bodies look. They may get their victims to mark their bodies with tattoos. The tattoo will be something that "honors" the somatic narcissist such as tattoos that say, "property of" and then the narcissist name. They may even pay for you

Love of Life

to get plastic surgery to fit how they want you to look. They are very critical of people's physical appearance.

Unlike the cerebral narcissist who is quite cold naturally, the somatic narcissist is hot. They love the warmth of another body next to them. They turn up the heat and scramble their victim's brains. Lust will be the sin that they are focused on, and physical touch will be the love language they will abuse. They may struggle with overindulgence and have a problem with porn and drugs. Gluttony and temperance are rooted in the body and the language of quality time will be abused by the somatic narcissist as well. They will isolate you from others or find people who appear isolated and secure and abuse them.

The narcissist, in general, chooses based on who they can get to satisfy the desires of their season. They tend to live double lives and will blame not living "their truth" due to acceptance, and no accountability for their false morality due to their sinful desires.

"And no wonder! Even Satan disguises himself as an angel of light. So it is not strange if his ministers also disguise themselves as ministers of righteousness. Their end will match their deeds."

(2 Corinthians 11:14)

True Love Never Ends

Love is not Earned

Unequally Yoked Equals Getting Choked

Be Neither Master Nor a Slave

Be Emotionally, and Spiritually Wealthy

Make it Don't Fake it

Relations Are Like Jobs, Produce Good Fruit

True Love Never Ends

"When I was a child, I spoke like a child, I thought like a child, I reasoned like a child; when I became an adult, I put an end to childish ways. For now we see in a mirror, dimly, but then we will see face to face. Now I know only in part; then I will know fully, even as I have been fully known. And now faith, hope, and love abide, these three; and the greatest of these is love."
(1 Corinthians 13:11-13)

    True love requires authenticity and connection. It is two of the prime factors that make unconditional love possible. Love respects boundaries and obeys the law of God. You must know love before you can recognize it properly. If you love someone and you do not love yourself, you will not be able to fully process when someone loves you. Some people get caught up in not loving themselves and look for others to do so, and some get too obsessed with loving themselves. When choosing to love another person romantically, you should operate like an expansion pack, not a life-line. Each person should have their own world that is better when joined with the other person. Your partner should be an extension of you that expands the love you already have. If that person is your world, they are your lifeline.

    Not everyone understands the concept of true love of self and God. There may be parts missing,

Love of Life

misfiring, or deactivated. In order to elect another individual as a lifeline, you would have to remove or shut off a part of themselves to operate. This is what stunts growth and promotes immaturity. All of which are ways to claim some your identity and corrupt their authenticity. Some people do not realize they have removed or deactivated a core part of themselves. They have been operating without it for so long they aren't able to discern a difference.

      Authenticity in identity is crucial and should not be surrendered to any human being. Identity should be surrendered to God. It is not a mood or a feeling; it is your discipline with your calling. Without it, you are a puppet, and a puppeteer can get its hands on you. Both the puppet and the puppeteer are losing due to commitment of illusion and the puppeteer is more likely to be aware of it. Nobody should accept being a puppet or puppeteer. This is how the master/slave dynamic operates, which is not to be confused with a leader/helper position in romantic love.

      Your spirit can corrupt your mind, and your mind can corrupt your spirit into assuming a different identity. The enemy's main goal is to corrupt your identity. This is created by false narratives and bad mental programming. This may occur outwardly too in the sense that someone else's mind or spirit can corrupt your being if given permission. Protect your authenticity and your

inherent goodness, and do not give access to permission to tarnish these elements.

Our first model of love is our parents. It is the model we are most likely to recreate in our lives. Familiarity breeds attachment and anything foreign may feel uncomfortable and can feel enemy worthy if it threatens the security of your previous attachment. Attachment levels are not indicators of true love but are an indicator of levels of stability. If you are unstable without someone then you have an unhealthy attachment. Unhealthy beliefs sustain unhealthy attachments. Beliefs, regardless of whether true or false can create strongholds. If beliefs are rooted in a false premise, no matter how good it feels – it will not be right.

Something right may not feel good due to a lack of familiarity. If someone is taught a false model, they may model It and wonder why they do not feel fulfilled. Or believe they are fulfilled but be confused or naïve to their own emptiness. True love never ends. If love appears to end, either it was a lie at the beginning or it was a lie at the end. Sadly, this tends to be a lie since the beginning, rather more so than a lie at the end.

Dysfunction causes corruption. It corrupts the very definition of what you may define as love. It can corrupt both the positive, and negative aspects of actions, thoughts, and behaviors. When you grow up in a broken from a toxic home, it is hard to discern what real love is.

Love of Life

Your baseline will always be what you know, and it's best for one to know better, but how can we know better if we see no different? We must be the difference we want to see in the world. When looking at why a family fell apart, it is important to assess what went wrong and discern what lessons and blessings you can gain from them.

All the negative assumptions that you perceive to be true should be challenged in the form of an optimal question. All positive assumptions should be challenged as well. For the negative, challenge it to see what good is possible. You never want to miss a good opportunity due to a lack of belief. Failure is a far better teacher than a false belief, but you will never know the difference if you do not try. False-positive assumptions can be blinding. Being naïve is not a positive trait - it is a limiting one. Being blind-sided by a negative event can be traumatizing.

What is true love?

"Set me as a seal upon your heart, as a seal upon your arm; for love is strong as death, passion fierce as the grave. Its flashes are flashes of fire, a raging flame. Many waters cannot quench love, neither can floods drown it. If one offered for love all the wealth of your house, it would be utterly scorned."
(Song of Solomon 8:6-7)

True Love Never Ends

Love is truly powerful. However, it can only be as powerful as your capabilities. Love should have ambition. Ambition plus character makes love powerful.

"To get wisdom is to love oneself; to keep understanding is to prosper."
(Proverbs 19:8)

If one does not understand what they possess, how are they to utilize it properly?

"Love never ends. But as for prophecies, they will come to an end; as for tongues, they will cease; as for knowledge, it will come to an end. For we know only in part, and we prophesy only in part but when the complete comes the partial will come to an end."
(1 Corinthians 13:8-1)

Love of Life

Lion and Lioness Love Code	
Lion	Lioness
"Show yourself in all respects a model of good works, and in your teaching show integrity, gravity, and sound speech that cannot be censured; then any opponent will be put to shame, having nothing evil to say of us." (Titus 2:7)	"She opens her mouth with wisdom and the teachings of kindness is on her tongue." (Proverbs 31:26)
"I hereby command you: Be strong and courageous; do not be frightened or dismayed, for the Lord your God is with you wherever you go." (Joshua 1:9)	"She perceives that her merchandise is profitable. Her lamp does not go out at night." (Proverbs 31:18)
"The heart of her husband trust in her, and he will have no lack of gain." (Proverbs 31:11)	"She does him good, and not harm, all the days of her life." (Proverbs 31:12)

"Husbands love your wives, just as Christ loved the church and gave himself up for her." (Ephesians 5:25)	"Strength and dignity are her clothing, and she laughs at the time to come." (Proverbs 31:25)
"In the same way, husbands should love their wives as they do their own bodies. He who loves his wife loves himself." (Ephesians 5:28)	"Her children rise up and call her happy; her husband too, and he praises her." (Proverbs 31:28)
"For this reason a man will leave his father and mother and be joined to his wife, and the two will become one flesh." (Ephesians 5:31)	"She looks well to the ways of her household, and does not eat the bread of idleness." (Proverbs 31:27)
"Husbands love your wives and never treat them harshly." (Colossians 3:19)	"Many women have done excellently, but you surpass them all." (Proverbs 31:29)

Love of Life

The One

There is an inherent need in all of us to feel chosen. There is a reason why in romantic love they say "I think I have found the one". When it comes to finding "the one" it is a matter of thought and a feeling much like that of an epiphany. The epiphany may come from the desires of the flesh or may come from God. It is best you have conversations with God as your consultant. People will have their opinions and visions of what they think you should have, but it may or may not be aligned with what God has for you.

If someone is "the one", they will have the three c's. They will connect with you, align with your calling, compliment you. Many people do not wait on God and end up in the wrong relationship. Many people find someone they like and ask God to honor them as "the one." God does honor the covenant of marriage; however, many Christians who end up divorced say they did not ask God whether they should date who they were formally married to. It's important to know God's voice separate from the desire of the flesh. It is an illusion that you have to earn being "the one" because it is a matter of recognition due to knowledge and not recognition due to action.

True Love Never Ends

A puzzle piece has four sides. Most people have four types of people they can connect with that they may identify as "the one". The left side puzzle piece connection represents a familiar love that doesn't allow you to move forward. They represent a connection you should leave behind. The relationship is a lot like a first love, it's immature and very imaginative. The puzzle piece that connects from the top represents someone you highly admire that can master you. That person on top will be treated as your God. The bottom part of your puzzle piece represents someone you can master as your slave. The puzzle piece facing to the right represents a person that is ultimately right for you. They align with your path moving forward in your calling.

Some people are edge puzzle pieces and will only have two to three matches as "the one." The people who are edge pieces that face left can only find immature matches or relationships where they are the master or slave. The upper right piece can only master people or find their immature match. The left edge puzzle piece types don't desire their immature match but may put someone above God or be someone else's God. No matter what piece you are, you can rotate and refine your edges to be who you are authentically meant to be. Let God shape you, and don't allow anyone to take you up, down, or left. Stay on the right track.

Love of Life

Unfortunately, if you do not ignite your true authentic self then you may be misidentified as "the one". It is critical to have your identity in line before joining forces with someone else because a false identity can be constructed to satiate someone else's needs and desires. It will be the will of the flesh and not the will of God. The will of God is suitable for you, the will of the devil is compatible with your dysfunction and immaturity. If you don't show and tell people who you are in your higher self, people will build and construct their own will for you in a way that benefits them. If that person who was constructed by another person starts to become their true self and it is contrary to what they perceived, they will feel deceived.

"He who finds a wife finds a good thing, and obtains favor from the Lord"
(Proverbs 18:22)

Men should seek out finding the one, women should be in position to be aligned with being found. A man should work on being a good finder and a woman should refine herself into a good find. We all have our divine assignments and it is between you and God how many you get. To receive our divine assignments, we must get into alignment with our highest selves. Some people are seasonal lessons in life, and "the one" maybe a yearly blessing in your life.

Think of the "the one" as a dream job, the ultimate job, the job you can happily see yourself with forever. The job that is your calling - did God call it or did you? There may be another dream job you have unforeseen if things do not work out. The more in tune you are with God, yourself and others, the more likely you are to be "right" when identifying who is right for you. If your mind is not right, or your spirit is not right, expect lies and confusion about who may be "the one" for you.

When a man meets a woman who he thinks is "the one," there is typically a shift in behavior that is not like that of the rest of the women he has sought out. A man can say he must date a woman who looks a certain way, or who lives only within a certain distance and say that he never wants to get married. However, that same man can meet "the one" and suddenly want to get married and compromise his "must-haves" because his original thoughts and behavior were based on his beliefs and not in his faith in what he wants. The shift makes men want to leave and cleave to his wife, and that shift is critical to whether the relationship is a fulfillment that will last. The same can go for a woman as well.

Love vs In Love

When you truly love yourself, you don't intentionally compromise yourself, and the same goes for when you are in love with someone. If you intentionally compromise them, then your love is conditional and simply not true. People don't fall out of love - they just realize they did not love in the first place. They fall out of love with a false dream. Unfortunately, a lot of people are selfish and are not connected to the person they are with. You can love multiple people, but you cannot be romantically in love with more than one person. Being in love involves full surrender. Once you are in love there is a oneness and that oneness prevents you from hurting that person intentionally. Their pain, their joy, is one with you. If you think you are in love with someone and you do not love yourself you will compromise the person you are with because they are one with you.

You cannot cheat on someone and be in love with them at the same time. If you choose to indulge in cheating it is an intentional action. You may have a love for them, but you are not in love with them because there has to be a disconnect to make such an action possible.

A happily married person might cheat on their spouse; just because someone is happy with you doesn't mean they are in love with you. Sometimes cheating is about happiness and sometimes it's about being disconnected. A connection to God, while having a connection with someone is vital in being faithful and honoring them. Without it, it is easy to fall (sin against them), and it doesn't make sense to maintain a relationship that is too hard to upkeep. It's not fulfilling to try to love someone who is not right for you. Whether or not you are caught compromising the relationship does not change whether or not you love them. Blinding someone is another step to not loving them, for you are not protecting them, you are protecting yourself.

      Women usually fall in love first, and men take a long time and usually don't fully fall in love until after they are married. A lot of men get stuck on fully falling in love which sometimes, unfortunately, wastes a woman's time (Medically there is an optimal time for women to have kids; God's time may be earlier or later than the statistically average). For a women's sake, it is best that men choose to get married when they have decided the woman is the one person they have the capacity to fully love, and to understand that falling fully in love is a process that will likely take them longer. Once you know who someone is, you should know what capacity you have to love them.

"Pursue love and strive for the spiritual gifts, and especially that you may prophesy."
(1 Corinthians 14)

Love is a calling, and we are to answer it when it is true.

"Love is patient; love is kind; love is not envious or boastful or arrogant or rude. It does not insist on its own way; it is not

Love of Life

irritable or resentful; it does not rejoice in wrongdoing, but rejoices in truth. It bears all things, believes all things, hopes all things, endures all things."
(1 Corinthians 13:4-7)

If one does not deliver or receive the message of love in this way, it cannot be true.

"Then Delilah said to him, "How can you say, 'I love you,' when you don't even trust me? This is the third time you have made a fool of me. You haven't told me the secret of your great strength."
(Judges 16:15) (NKJ)

Trust is key. For if there is no truth there is no true love.

"But speaking the truth in love, we must grow up in every way into him who is the head, into Christ."
(Ephesians 4:15)

It is not humble to be selfless; it falls short of grace. Self-deprecation is the condemnation of self, and conviction is the truth laced with responsibility. It's the difference between "I'm bad" and "I did something bad, I will try to do better next time". It is best to assume responsibility, then it is to assume an identity. Assuming identity based on an act renders you powerless to it, and responsibility empowers you.

True Love Never Ends

"I do not judge anyone who hears my words and does not keep them, for I came not to judge the world, but to save the world"
(John 12:47)

Love is not Earned

"It's not about deserve, it's about what I believe. And I believe in love"
- Wonder Woman

    The paradoxical issue of saying someone deserves or doesn't deserve you implies that you need to be earned. By saying that we immediately set a precedent of superiority and inferiority. You are not supposed to earn love. You are supposed to search for an equal match; one that harmonizes with each other's authenticity to flourish in life. A needy person is selfless and will over-invest, a narcissistic person will think there are above everyone else and therefore underinvest. This is how a narcissistic person and a selfless person become a match. It is the relationship between a drug dealer and an addict. The results of their relationship may look like love. They may look like they have real fruit. However, you must discern between fruit and artificial flavoring.

    A love quote that implies a toxic lesson, "People accept the love they think they deserve." Love is not about seeking validation. At times, people accept less than they should due to low self-esteem. Low self-esteem puts people into the mentality of "beggars can't be choosers." A beggar has the propensity to humiliate humility. Rather than combating negativity on themselves, they will side with the negativity, and then

Love of Life

ponder why they deserved it.

People may say all the right words and appear to do all the right things. A candy strawberry may look and taste strawberry-like but it will give you a cavity, unlike real strawberries. Artificial flavoring in relationships can have cancerous properties that create an unhealthy bond that tends to lead to obsession, depression, and destruction. Obsession is created by a lack of security. If someone is insecure, they will want an extreme to make them feel safe. If someone was cheated on, and they were traumatized by it, they may want someone who is obsessed with them so that cheating may not be a possibility. They were hurt so badly that they wanted to make being hurt again impossible. An anxious person typically did not grow up in a safe environment, and their boundaries were constantly crossed and violated. An avoidant partner also did not grow up in a safe environment and fears abandonment.

A narcissist will slip a drug called love into your drink and rape your potential for a healthy happy life. The drug dealer is only focused on their goals and is not concerned about the damage they do to your wallet, mind, or body. The addict is concerned with feeding a fixation. Like an unhealthily obsessed fan of a celebrity, there is no equal playing ground. At times it may be the fan who is covertly narcissistic and trying to master the celebrity. They may act like their best friend, feeding them compliments, and following them in "support" when really, they want to consume every fiber of the celebrity's being. They want their time, their wealth, and their friendship, and if they don't get it there will be hell to pay. A "humble" celebrity may fall for this and think the person is not their fan but their friend. A celebrity may do the same to their fans and drain them. No matter your level, higher or lower you may be drained from narcissism.

People in narcissistic selfless relationships; have a people pleaser who is selfless and gives actions of love (codependent), and a counterpart who selfishly seeks validation by receiving love (narcissist). People who have healthy self-esteem do not try to validate themselves through others, they simply look for the right fit. They look at others as a puzzle piece that either clicks or doesn't click. They do not look at themselves with others as if they are supposed to be blended together like soup. The ingredients of their identity are not meant to be mixed with other people making it hard to identify original sources of being. If a relationship is not the right fit, do not force it. A puzzle piece is a solid piece and a solid individual is solid in their own peace.

The narcissist will always be the base of the relationship like noodles to a soup, and the selfless will always be the one pouring in ingredients trying to alter it to the base's satisfaction. Unhealthy relationships have magnetism. It is two people drawn to each other that

Love of Life

cling to one another. Puzzle pieces do not operate this way; they click rather than cling to each other. This makes the outer world of life make more sense, rather than creating their own isolated world separate from everything and everyone else. In this life, it's best to make real-life so good that fantasy seems like child's play.

Since love is not supposed to be earned, it is wise not to need the phrases "thank you" or "I'm sorry." If you need someone to say thank you, the action must have been an expense to you. If "I'm sorry" is needed, this states that "I want you to pay for what you have done, so I no longer have to pay for it." Love forgives a multitude a sin's and therefore makes love debt free. Be debt-free - do not pay too much and expect nothing in return. This is not to say nobody should take accountability or give back. The best "I'm sorry" is changed behavior, the best "thank you" is not wasting what was given. You may say "thank you" and say "I'm sorry," just do not need them personally to function.

Narcissists love to mirror behavior to seduce you. If your partner is too agreeable with you that it is a red flag. The phrase "me too" will be your main bonding agent. If you do an action, they may mirror it. If you take a trip, they may take a better trip to assert their superiority, which would be an abuse of gifts love language. They may even do just a bit less to assert their superiority as well or match efforts to neutralize you

Love is Not Earned

having any power. Love is in what someone says and does, and the why makes all the difference.

If you believe that love is about what someone deserves, and about being earned, you will certainly take on the role of a narcissist or a selfless person. The love of your life will have a positive influence and drive you to be a better person. Like the piece of a puzzle, when matched it will help you to identify and illuminate what is around you and help you build other aspects of your life. You are a match if you are resonating with your calling in life.

Love is a distinct choice and investment. There are good investments and bad investments. If your authentic self depreciates in value, then you should end the relationship and reassess what made you susceptible to a diabolical match. Fantasy is not fulfilling; you will face reality, and it will hurt beyond your imagining. Illusions are sought when your reality is not good, if reality is great then fantasy is simply a distraction from what is good.

Love is not supposed to be earned; trust is supposed to be earned. When encountering someone to possibly date and marry you should focus on trust. Check their character and let them earn good standing. Trust is earned not deserved.

Unequally Yoked Equals Getting Choked

"Do not be mismatched with unbelievers. For what partnership is there between righteousness and lawlessness? Or what fellowship is there between light and dark?"
(II Corinthians 6:14)

The term equally yoked refers to a cow being linked to another cow by the neck. If you have both cows indicating directions there will be friction, and you will get nowhere fast. You are to operate as one, and in a way, one leads in whatever position they assume.

"But from the beginning of creation, God made them male and female. For this reason a man shall leave his father and mother and be joined to his wife, and the two shall become one flesh. Therefore what God has joined together, let no one separate."
(Mark 10:6-9)

Being equally yoked as a lot to do with being equal in terms of your beliefs. If you are not equally yoked, both will suffer consequences. If one is ambitious and the other is not towards a particular plan, one will be a drag or be dragged if they go towards it. A lot of people make the mistake that the proper solution is to stay still rather than dragging, instead of reconsidering.

Love of Life

whether the person is meant to be with you. The problem is either your purpose or your partner. The answer is involved in the revaluation of purpose. What is the purpose of the will? Does that will take away from God's will for you? If God has called you to become something, he will not send you someone to counteract that. If you chose the person you are with, instead of what God has called you to do, then you have made that person your God.

If you don't know what God has called you to do, how can you know who God has called to be your husband or wife? One cannot agree or disagree with something if they do not know what it is. If you do not know who you are there is no telling who you are supposed to be with. If you think you do know who you want to spend the rest of your life with, and you do not know who you are then your identity will be in the person you are dating and not in Christ. Once you know who you are it is pretty clear who you are supposed to take with you. If you surrender your identity to anyone other than God, you will be in for one hell of a ride. Only a master looking for a slave will desire someone without an identity to marry.

If you are a match for each other your purposes you will divinely align. Once you have told yourself your purpose in life is to be with someone and it overrides the works you are supposed to produce you have lost your

Unequally Yoked Equals Getting Choked

way. If you do not feel you have a purpose, you will try to find ways to feel good as you long for meaning. People with a master mentality may try to give you meaning by giving you titles such as husband/wife. You know you have the power of self-respect when you can leave a situation that doesn't serve you. People who say marriage is a trap likely didn't know the person they are with or did not know themselves. If you are with the right person it is an acceleration in life, not a derailment.

When it comes to age, most women and men are mature by their late twenties. It is not recommended that you marry before you are mature, because maturity can breed a whole new person. Also, it's not recommended to date anyone who can be old enough to be your parent, or young enough to be your child. The generation gap may create an authoritative difference due to age that makes not being equally yoked possible. It's best to date people within your own generation and to try to avoid any gap more than ten years apart once you are in your thirties.

When it comes to marriage, you want someone you can cooperate with to make you better. You do not want to lag or make yourself dull. Many people think that if there is at least some movement, that's all you need. God does not put someone in our life to slow down our purpose. The enemy does. The advantage of maturity is

Love of Life

that you have something to offer. God sends people, and so does the devil.

"Therefore, since we are surrounded by so great a cloud of witnesses, let us also lay aside every weight and the sin that clings so closely, and let us run with perseverance the race that is set before us."
(Hebrews 12:1)

Not having self-esteem and picking a mate is like being drunk and deciding to make important life decisions. It is not likely you are going to make good decisions, and with sober judgment, you are more likely to make decisions in your best interest. Be wary of those who prefer you drunk. If they congratulate your fall, encourage your fall, neglect and or insult you for falling leave them. If someone leaves you because you start walking righteously, then their mission was not to love you. You should question the person who does not like you with a pure heart, mind, body, and soul. The person who likes you drunk will captivate you with your weaknesses. What do they activate in you? Good or evil?

"Wives, be subject to your husbands as you are to the Lord."
(Ephesians 5:22)

A lot of people mistake the husband/wife role as a master/slave relationship. It is not a master and slave relationship; it is a leader and helper. One is not superior

Unequally Yoked Equals Getting Choked

to the other. Providing is not supreme to nurturing or vice versa. People at times abuse their power which creates a master/slave dynamic. It is not true that the helper is a slave to the leader, or that the helper is a master over the leader. As long as there is no abuse of power there will be a balance. A lot of people have been victims of abuse of power; however, the solution is not in changing the way God meant for us to be. Doing so will ultimately breed more pride, unhappiness, and disconnection from God.

"Husbands love your wives, just as Christ loved the church and gave himself up for her."
(Ephesians 5:25)

What Christ did for the church is a huge showcase of love. Understand your sexual differences and do not notate them as superior or inferior. There may be more work than you may be able to perceive when it comes to the opposite sex and their roles. The positions are different, and trying to equalize them won't bring balance it will bring illusion. If you call a wolf in sheep's clothing a sheep you have already lost the battle of truth and have subscribed to delusion. It may make the wolf feel better to be called a sheep but you are doing an injustice. Once you put a wolf in sheep's clothing among other sheep and tell other sheep that it is a sheep you have now endangered them. The wolf will eventually act out like a wolf, and if you have sheep thinking the wolf is like them, they may adopt the wolf's behavior as well and be

Love of Life

confused by their very identity. Corruption of truth is the ultimate seduction to falling from grace.

"Be subject to one another out of reverence for Christ."
(Ephesians 5:21)

Many will select the passage from the bible about women being subject to their husbands and forget Ephesians 5:21. Context matters, and it's important to know the word for yourself. It is not a one-way street, both husband and wife are to be subject to one another. Only approximately forty six percent of children in 2019 are raised by both parents. It is important before things begin to understand how some end. Grounds for divorce in Christianity include adultery and abandonment.

7 grounds for fault in divorce (most laws in the United States.)

Adultery

Domestic violence

Bigamy

Cruelty

Abandonment

Uncommon Grounds

Long-term imprisonment

Unequally Yoked Equals Getting Choked

7 Uncommon grounds for divorce

Alcohol or substance abuse

Impotency

Infertility

Incompatible sexuality

Cultural or religious differences

Financial

Mental abuse

No-fault divorce is commonly listed as "irreconcilable differences." Typically, the couple didn't know each well or grew apart overtime. Sometimes people commit to living a lie. Once they are tired of living the lie the relationship ends. People do not like to believe their happiest moments were in a lie. They may be confused and look at wedding photos and think they both look the happiest they have ever been. They would rather believe the "new" person they see is a lie because the truth makes them miserable. Letting go of good memories is exceptionally difficult. Usually, when people file for divorce, they checkmark "irreconcilable differences," and those differences may be in fantasy vs reality. Your differences in a partnership are supposed to complement each other, and if the differences are irreconcilable then their love was conditional. Those conditions may be based on how much you tell and live the truth.

When you do not honor and respect each other there is no order. If there is no order there is chaos which creates a lack of honor and respect. If you are free to do anything to someone whether it is intentionally good or evil, that freedom tends to foster disrespect. You will not want to honor someone who disrespects you. People make mistakes; however, if those mistakes are not intentional, there will be a desire to forgive and hopefully improve.

Willpower will allow for improvement, but if you do not have willpower then you are consumed by something other than love. That something can be a compulsion that stems from addiction. A person who is consumed by addiction is not whole in themselves, which means they cannot wholly love you. It is dangerous to be with someone who lacks ambition and has low self-esteem because there will be nothing to work with once you have problems.

Be Neither Master Nor Slave

Beware of power struggles – these are clear indications that you do not love each other. Even if one of you has surrendered, it is a losing game. One of the signs of a great leader is ambition. If a man has no desire to lead, he doesn't have a true vision of himself aligned with God. If a woman has no desire to help, she too is not aligned with God and may feed the illusion of the fairytale that she needs to be saved because she feels helpless. We may develop the immature thoughts of a child. A man may think like a boy and say to himself "I have no desire to lead, I want someone else to lead me," and a woman who thinks like a little girl may say, "I have no desire to help, help me."

A mature person will take responsibility and won't want to be babied. In feeling helpless, the helper may falsely try to empower herself by being a leader. A man may also try to falsely empower himself by being a helper. Leaders are not control freaks or masters, and helpers are not meant to be people-pleasers or slaves. Control freaks have pride, and people-pleasers have an unhealthy form of humility. Control freaks orchestrate as master manipulators. People-pleasers may not always be emotionally aware of the control because of

Love of Life

their unhealthy form of humility blinds them from the truth.

Relationships should not be out of control and it doesn't mean that nobody should be pleased. Your partner should be someone you can bargain with, if you cannot say no to them then you are a slave. It has a lot to do with mutual desire, respect, consent, and trust in one another's positions and abilities. A good relationship helps you grow. A leader wants a helper, a helper wants a leader. If a leader is with a people pleaser (unhealthy helper) he will have nothing to contend with which hinders his ability to grow and makes him dull overtime. In that dullness, he will lose attraction for her over time, if not immediately. If a helper finds a control freak (unhealthy leader) she will feel restricted, lose attraction and may even tell him to help himself and leave him.

A man not wanting to lead may want to be controlled, and a woman not wanting to help may want to be the controller. Both illusions are compatible with one another in their brokenness and unrighteousness. It may appear to work, as it is both their new dream stemming from a traumatic wound. Maybe the woman was in a position with an abusive leader and now no longer trusts or believes a man can lead her. Perhaps, the man had a helper who didn't help him but hurt him. He may give up on himself and let her madness to lead the way.

Be Neither Master Nor Slave

If we become aware that our dream is built on an illusion that is reinforcing our traumatic wound then we can reclaim our power. We are to operate from our peace and not our pain. Once the illusion is broken, we may have resentment towards our partner and or ourselves. We may lose of respect for ourselves and or for them. We may have compassion as well due to understanding that you were both hurt trying to make the best of a new dream that was a false reality. The creation of a false identity is due to the hatred of self, hatred of others, or hatred of God. Not believing in each other's positions in terms of leader and helper may cause conflict and misidentification in Christ. Being subject to one another is an honor when you have a partner you respect.

Helping is an honor when someone is exceptional and respectable. Leading someone who is a great help is a blessing. We are all created in Christ's image. Living a lie leads us away from God, and the disconnect from God's will causes corrosion of the heart and soul. While trying to create a new image other than God's, you deconstruct who you are authentically, which causes disharmony. The cure for the emasculation of a man is not feminization, the cure for defeminization of a woman is not masculinization.

Imagine a relationship as a car and a relationship as one person. As a provider, a man may lead direction

Love of Life

by utilizing the wheel; as a nurturer a woman may help by pushing the gas pedal. Women usually manage the speed of the relationship and men dictate direction. There is a reason why women worry about being too fast, or men worry about not having a direction in life.

Typically, a man will be the wheel as he is to lead, and a woman will be the pedal. However, be prepared to shift positions if it serves for the betterment of the progress of the relationship. Men and women both lead in whatever position they assume to help one another. Being with someone can hold you back or propel you. If there is an imbalance there will be no drive or an uneasy drive. If someone's energy is propelling you to a direction in which you may not want to proceed, you may swerve off that road and never get to your destination. If someone is going a direction you do not agree with you may refuse to submit any energy to the pedal and be dead weight.

If two people are leaders or two people are helpers, a master and slave dynamic will be inevitable. It is impossible to join together and be one. One of you would have to delude yourself to assume the other position. Master manipulators focus on goals that people can do for them absent of satisfying other people's needs, while a slave supplier focuses on goals that they can do for other people absent of what they need for themselves. It makes being equally yoked impossible, and true love is unattainable due to false identity. One person will always dominate in the driver's seat, and two cannot sit in one seat comfortably and be efficient. You may still get to a destination while switching from the pedal or wheel, but underneath the surface, there will always be something missing. A bond can be created, but not a divine connection. Not everyone will be intuitive enough to know dysfunction especially if they appear the get "similar" results.

  Real love has a challenge because it has a purpose, and in our purpose, we level up on the way. If someone doesn't want a challenge then they want a pushover, which would require a master/slave dynamic. The term "love is love" is deceptive. If you were to ask someone "Is this a donut?" and someone says "a donut is a donut" would you trust them? It is important to note the true properties involved in true love. People may call things what they want, but the truth will discern if you have chosen a healthy reality or a deceptive fantasy.

  Yes, as an individual you may lead and give fuel to your own being and desires. But there are certain things you cannot do entirely on your own. Creating a child is one of them. Two become one. When children die, the parents' relationship has a higher chance of failure because an example of what made them one is now gone. When joining forces, roles should be clear and assist toward the betterment of both individuals. When

Love of Life

you talk with your partner does it feel like a conversation or an interview? Power struggles are governed by fear and resentment. If you are trying to own each other then this is an indicator of possession, which is coupled with obsession, and equals an unhealthy attachment.

What creates a power struggle is when either the leader or the helper ends up abusing their power. That's when the leader helper dynamic switches into a master/slave dynamic. The power struggle created resentment. "I do not need you" or "what are you good for?" are often questions that occur when one partner feels unjustified. Many people feel the resolve is in making the positions the same. The positions are not the same, and both are needed for their distinct differences. A woman cannot have a baby in her stomach for four and a half months and transfer it to a man to carry the rest of the term.

"Above all, maintain constant love for one another, for love covers a multitude of sins."
(1 Peter 4:8)

Marriage is a sacrament. A sacrament is a visible sign of an inward grace. We may fall from grace with our vices, and it's important to rise to our virtues. This is hard for those who have a hero complex and whose primary love language is acts of service. The hero can feel happy saving someone else. This may appear fulfilling but can

drain you if you are saving a person who should be saving themselves.

It is equally yoked to have an ally in marriage. A leader and helper dynamic, not a leader and someone who needs to be helped. Not all that is equal is fair, and not all that is fair is equal in the sense of being the same. The goal is fairness. If men and women are fair to each other, the positions they serve will not be offensive to each other. The positions are only offensive if they are not served well respectfully.

Play into each other's strengths. If you have to switch positions to get to a destination, don't hesitate to help or to lead. Both men and women should be able to play both parts in terms of their abilities within their design. Meaning, you should not be rigid on with gender roles such as "only women do the dishes" or "only men should be allowed to work." These are cultural standpoints and not biblical ones. Both sexes are able to do both, but do what works to your advantages. If a man must go to work, and the woman must stay home to breastfeed and take care of the baby - there is nothing wrong with that. We should not resent the limits of our design, or feel superior due to the ability of our design.

If life is a play, both people are main characters and at times one person may be supporting or leading the scene. In a play, if you are given a certain role because of your design and the other person told you, "I cannot play my role, can you play your role and my own?" Can you imagine how frustrated and angry would you be? If you hate your role it will be hard to connect with others which is why it's best to accept who you are.

It's hard to honor and respect a man who is emasculated, or a woman who insults her femininity. We both lead in whatever position we play and we both should be supporting characters to one another's position. Be able, and be stable in your identity in Christ. Do your best, and be full so others may not have to fill your position.

"The place for which He designs human beings in His scheme of things is the place they are made for. When we want to be something other than the thing God wants us to be, we must be wanting what, in fact, will not make us happy."

C. S. Lewis

Be Emotionally and Spiritually Wealthy

"The rich rule over the poor, and the borrower is the slave of the lender."
(Proverbs 22:7)

Be so wealthy that it is not expensive for you to give, kindness, forgiveness, or charity. It is only expensive if it is beyond what you can afford. If you are giving to get, you are in a vulnerable position that is unfavorable even if you do receive it. Give without needing to receive, and treat what you give as a donation or an investment. Donations and investments are reflective around time and money.

If you are wealthy and you give a friend in need $2.00 that they never payback it will not be a big deal financially because you are abundant. The principle of them not paying you back may upset you, but you will not feel a draught because you didn't give above your means of survival. If by giving the $2.00, you starve the next day because you cannot afford food, you will feel that loss to its core. You will have suffered for giving above your means. The rich may give to the poor in order to assert the power over them. Not knowing or honing your power will allow you to abuse yourself or be abused by others.

When creating a partnership, what you give will be an investment. You can lie to yourself in a romantic relationship and say it's just a donation, but if something takes the majority of your time it is an investment whether you like it or not. Wise investments are of equally yoked substance. Be abundant in treasure and devoid of waste. If you are wasteful, you may lead yourself to be susceptible to unhealthy bonds.

There is a reason why when addicts leave rehab and heal, they usually change their friends and romantic relationships. They truly were not themselves at the times they were under the influence. After healing they matured their habits and their palettes to find the truth. What they thought they needed wasn't really what they wanted. When one is of sober judgment and in support of their better selves, toxins are naturally unattractive and intolerable. Even if the people around them didn't enable their drug use, it is unattractive to them that you tolerated their behavior. If you were once a slob and you knew that those around you loved you being a slob, you will wonder if their judgment was as impaired as yours once was when you were a slob. If they loved you despite being a slob you may also wonder if they have unconditional love

Be Emotionally and Spiritually Wealthy

for you. You may not understand unconditional love if you only have conditional love for yourself.

If you believe someone was attracted to you because of your toxins, you may not respect them for their poor palate to desire you. Sober people are trying to renew their minds, and not be reminded of their old one as they move forward. Not everyone is judgmental, but when someone heals, they have to establish new healthy boundaries. The best way to establish new healthy boundaries is to start from scratch and slowly introduce things and or people into your life. As one grows in being spiritually wealthy one should be charitable, and preserve what is precious. Be selective with investments. What you indulge nourishes or destroys you, if you do not indulge you will starve to ashes and by default destroy.

"For you say, 'I am rich, I have prospered, and I need nothing.' You do not realize that you are wretched, pitiable, poor, blind, and naked. Therefore I counsel you to buy from me gold refined by fire so that you may be rich; and white robes to clothe you and to keep the shame of your nakedness from being seen; and salve to anoint your eyes so that you may see."
(Revelations 3:17-18)

As you watch and admire other people's power do not forget to hone your own. You can use it to be manipulative, or innovative. Manipulating someone to

feel good about something that is false is not right. We are not to manipulate how people feel. If you truly care about someone you tell them the truth and you help them innovate. One can be tempting or inspiring. Manipulators are effective communicators, and Innovators are effective communicators. It is vital to be an effective communicator to achieve fulfillment and interconnectedness. One can be good and be an Innovator, or one can be bad and be a manipulator. The flow will either increase or decrease your emotional, and spiritual wealth. Here are some key differences between a manipulator and an innovator:

Be Emotionally and Spiritually Wealthy

Manipulator	Innovator
Charming and Self Serving	Captivating and God Serving
Negative Influence	Positive Influence
Operates from Blame and Shame	Operates in Responsibility & Accountability
Goal-oriented in Pride (Get's disconnected in sin)	Goal-Oriented in Humility (Get's connected in virtue)
Works Illusions	Works Miracles
Opponent strategist	Co-op supporter
Bad intentions	Good intentions

"The discerning heart seeks knowledge, while the fool feeds on trash."
(Proverbs 15:14)(NIV/NLT).

Loving someone is not about manipulation, it is about innovation in each other's lives. Being an innovator and reading the Bible helps one gain spiritual wealth. Spiritual wealth is in innovation through our words and our works. Emotional wealth is in living a balanced life, which includes fulfilling basic human needs such as sleeping, eating right, and exercising your mind, body, and soul in routine maintenance. Both tie into being wealthy which is fruitful to your life and others. People

Love of Life

talk about being wealthy in finances, but we must not neglect emotional and spiritual wealth.

Make it, Don't Fake it

Maintenance in the discipline of your principles will build character. Building competence breeds confidence. Do not judge the levels you are at; simply be dedicated to leveling up. Failure is not doom; it is part of the process. Think of life as a video game - you may not win at every level perfectly, but even if you fail you may get a shot to continue and try again. If you can no longer access certain levels try other ones and build up.

Truth is of utmost importance. Be impeccable with your word, but do not feel the need to hold on to it if the premise is untrue, or wicked. If one makes a promise and it turns out to be on a false or wicked premise, they should no longer keep it. If the premise is fraudulent then the promise is void. It is hard to end something that appears to have good results when the source is fake. There are plenty of stories where people appeared to have gained great things by being fake. However, the emptiness is a black hole and no matter how much you feed it, nothing real can be held on to in a way that is true. No illusion will ever be supreme to truth and love. It doesn't even compare, and no one should compare it. Counterfeit is not true currency. Never be jealous of it, honor it, or treat it as true.

If someone's identity is a lie, their love is as well. The person who is being fake knows they were being

Love of Life

fake so they see any love they receive as foolery. If someone calls you stupid or a fool for loving them you should evaluate how much you have been deceived or how much that person deceives themselves for being a loveable person. If they are willing to say you're a fool or stupid for loving them, then there is no way that they love you.

Think of an actor. If you met a person in real life and talked to them as if they were the character they portrayed in a film, how do you think they would perceive you? If someone loves themselves, they will not be someone else to seduce you. Are the people in your life being genuine in their actions of love towards you? In which case they would not see your love as foolishness. Only a disingenuous person or someone who doesn't love themselves would see you loving them as foolish. You can buy someone things, you can cook for them, you can say the right things, you can give them time, and you can be good in bed. It will not guarantee you love.

People fall in love based on the authenticity of your character and anything else is an illusion. If someone "falls in love" with you based on what you do for them, expect their love to be conditional. Some individuals will look for someone who can fill their needs, and who they choose may not be what they want. It's best to be on the wanted list, then the needed list. You cannot be on the wanted list if you don't make something of yourself, and you don't want to be on the needed list because that will be a drain for you.

A lot of people make the mistake of saying you need to find someone you need in hopes that you will eventually want them. This is poor advice, don't find what you need, fill your own needs in terms of being whole as an individual. Nobody who loves their spouse will complain about being too wanted, but they may complain about a person being too needy. The phrase "I need you," may indicate a reflection of poor health.

Manipulators prefer needy people. People who don't know love and confuse it with obsession will want a needy looking relationship. When you are not whole as an individual, needs are a priority and wants are a minority of your decisions. What one identifies as "needs" will all be lies if you have low self-esteem. "I need you for stability" or "I need you so I can be a happy person." People may not be so honest with themselves. They may say "I need stability" and then go seek their significant other for it when they should secure it within themselves.

At a base, two people should want each other. If someone wants you to fulfill needs that they should be filling themselves, they are looking for a master/slave situation. It is a cruel thing to be needed by someone who doesn't want you. If you want someone bad and not right for you, you need to figure out in yourself why you may

diabolically desire destruction. Do not figure out how to want someone you should "need."

People fall into unhealthy relationships at times to fill their identity. They want to become a mom or dad; they want to be a husband or a wife. These roles revolve around identity. They may compromise their desires just to have the title because it is very important to them. Sometimes this is as a result of coming from a broken family. Especially in cases of divorce. It's difficult when what made you whole gets ripped apart. If your parent's divorce they may question if real love is possible. At times people try to escape and "fix" their past by creating a future that is contrary to it. They may inevitably recreate their past because they did not want to learn a lesson and wanted an immediate blessing cover their hurt and pain. They may get married for the wrong reasons, or they may not ever marry or believe in marriage since their parent's relationship failed.

If you don't know who you are, a person may try to create who you are to serve their needs. Not knowing who you are makes you optimal for a slave position. There is nothing like being authentic and receiving blessings. You may be alone, but it will always be better than having the wrong person. The wrong person will stunt your growth. You cannot say they really lived life if all the memories you have are with an imaginary friend.

Make it Don't Fake it

Being bored without works can produce fantasy. The longer you are in fantasy, the harder and weirder it is to adjust to reality. Drug addicts wouldn't be addicts if they had no desire to escape reality in the first place. Make your reality so good that it makes it the risk of temptation hard to entertain. Make your reality so great, that you look like the ultimate expansion for someone else.

Make decisions based on authenticity, not based on desired results. Make it, don't fake it, and prepared for evil to want to take it, and break it. You should not repress good qualities but protect them. Protect the truth and do not give in to illusions. There is goodness in the belief of worthiness, and in possibilities. Believing in yourself is crucial to having a fulfilling life. Instead of fake it, believe in it and create it. Live life as it was a movie. If you have confidence in the end of it, no matter what happens at the beginning or middle of the movie you will not worry. Accept the truth, put your energy into growth, have faith in your authentic self as opposed to fear, and you will be okay with the result of any contest. Put all negative assumptions the form of a question and challenge them: It's the only way to achieve unforeseen goodness. All positive assumptions should be researched for clear evidence, it's the only way to not be deceived.

Relationships Are Like Jobs, Produce Good Fruit

A job is supposed to have a purpose. This is not the employee, and employer dynamic. A relationship has two people who are equally yoked and expanding in emotional wealth. Two brands of authentic people joining together to make goodness. If the collaboration ends and it feels like one of you got fired, then you know you had an unequally yoked relationship. Relationships don't have to be hard work but should garner interdependence in a way that is fruitful for flourishing in life.

If you have your dream job, work will feel like you play for a living. It may be a challenging game but it's worth every minute. You play your true calling in harmony with peace and goodness. There may be bumps in performance but you will love it so much that the mistakes will not be the focus

Mind, body, spirit, and soul should be nourished on an individual level and your counterpart should be your expansion, not your lifeline to your emotional wealth. Your body tells the truth more than the words you may tell yourself. Your mind can rationalize an unhealthy relationship, but your body will always show you the damage. What you show will have more weight than what you tell. If you're anxious, sick, or constantly tired, fearful, and confused it's time to evaluate.

It is important to take note while studying love language that you study your own body language as well. Do you expand or contract when mentioning this person? What is your tempo in speech? Does the volume turn down? Is the beat peaceful and or happy? Is your breath shallow? Are you drained after going to them? When they contact you, are you delighted to hear from them? Is that delight a drug-like high, or is it spiritually peaceful and happy? Are you looking for a way out instead of having more curiosity to get into them? Is your partnership authentic?

People are like jobs. A man may be a leader interviewing to find a helper, and a helper may be an interviewee looking for the right job. As an interviewee one should be interviewing their employer, it is not a one-way street. Both get to choose each other. After the interview the man should call if interested. A woman may call to get the job, however the switch in roles may create a new dynamic that may not be in each other's favor. If the woman calls, she is saying "I really want you above the rest" and doing so will only be a good thing if the woman failed to showcase her desire at the time of interview. Remember, he who finds a wife finds a good

thing. If he has found a good thing she will not have to say "here I am" he'll recognize it. A woman should be about her father's business.

"And He said to them, "Why did you seek Me? Did you not know that I must be about My Father's business?"
(Luke 2:49)

Being anxious and not allowing room for a person to decide in due time may showcase desperation which shows that person may be in a state of lack. Being in a state of lack is not attractive. If the passenger has to start the engine, what's going with the driver? Is he taking too long? Did the passenger not trust the driver? Or did the driver not really want the passenger?

Women should have their foot on the brake and wait for the man to start the car. If you have to drag or force someone to go with you somewhere, that may be the first sign a partnership will fail. Always work on being confident enough to be able to quit if it isn't right. Men start the engine if you are ready to go, ladies don't take your foot off the brake if you do not want to go anywhere. Always work on being confident enough in your position and not want to take over the other person's role.

Titles are important because they reflect allowance. Titles also show how much you honor or respect them. Your calling should come before your title.

Love of Life

Some people are looking for temp positions, some full-time or part-time. Keep in mind nobody should govern you; you don't work under them and they do not work under you. There is no boss and employee dynamic because master-slave dynamics will ensue inevitably on those grounds. The positions that support equally yoked situations are duel independent contractors and partners.

Independent contractors are boyfriend/girlfriend and partners are married couples. There are interviewers, and a date is a meeting between two interviewers. To say you are dating is to say you are interviewing each other. If a conversation feels like a one-sided interview you are not mutually applying. All other positions are fulfilling needs without obligation of reciprocation. One may not even have or want a title and simply come for benefits. If you are getting benefits and are fulfilling none of the person's requirements you are selfish; if you are giving requirements and reap no benefits you are selfless.

Some people are not looking for partnerships, but it doesn't mean they do not want benefits. Don't give a temp or a part-timer partnership responsibilities and benefits. If they slack, they can easily say that it isn't their job, and they are right. Also, in doing so, it cheapens the advancement of the partnership title. If people can do less and get more, they will. One cannot expect motivation if there are no advancements for an upgrade.

Relationships Are Like Jobs

Track records matter and people who have once occupied the position may seemingly increase or decrease what that person thinks is the value of said position. Requirements are elements needed to sustain your title; benefits are what you both receive mutually.

Independent contractors include emotional support, honor, respect, and acknowledgment. Both independent contractors have their own lives. Their lives are not one. They plan dates and plan times so that they can see each other despite their busy individual schedules. When introduced to other people, they are acknowledged as boyfriend/girlfriend. There are boundaries that showcase honor and respect, and access is limited but each other's works in one another's life is respected.

In the confines of an independent contract (boyfriend/girlfriend) physical touch may include holding hands, cuddling, and kissing. Some people refrain from kissing until marriage. However, keep in mind being able to wait for a long time may be an indicator of lack of interest or sexual issues. If someone is "the one" waiting for years to kiss when you are a mature adult may be an indicator of a problem. Making out leads to having sex, and most people do not have the discipline to stop themselves. Waiting till marriage to have sex is going to be a challenge when you meet "the one". What shouldn't be a challenge is whether or not you want to marry them

Love of Life

after you recognize each other authentically as "the one". In which case, you won't be "waiting till marriage" you will be planning to marry because it makes no sense to wait once you know. Once you've made up your mind you don't need a timer to make a selection. Your sense of planning in accordance to time will be external (booking a wedding venue for example may not be immediately available and you may have to wait) not internal (uncertainty in your mind, body, spirit, or soul. "The one" resonates with your mind, body, spirit, and soul and anything else is not the one God has for you). If it is not a challenge to wait; you may not be a right fit for each other. Set boundaries with yourself and be honest about the circumstances that may compromise them. Independent contract is not meant to last for a long period of time. Finances are used for activities together, and not for each other's independent bills, or living expenses. Just as access is limited, so are requirements. They are not required to spend the holidays with you or to spend the night.

      Partnerships are when two independents become interdependent. They become each other's expansion packs. Expansion packs include everything from the independent contractor's pack and more. It is no longer your world or my world, but our world. The expansion benefits include sex, living together, babies, holidays, trips, and joint finances,

Relationships Are Like Jobs

In terms of benefits, many people will give benefits before titles. If one gives someone benefits without titles, they run the risk of being disrespected. Someone who only fulfills requirements with few benefits will also get disrespected. It's like working for free or acquiring free money without work. Only a narcissist will want to master someone they can order around (acquire free money); only a selfless person will want to hold a slave position and be told what to do (work for free). A selfless person has an unhealthy form of humility, a narcissist has pride. Pride and humility are opposites, but when humility is sick the positive becomes a "negative" while turning pride from a negative to a "positive," creating a diabolical magnetic match.

Order matters and presentation matters. If one sees you are doing things out of order, they will lack the desire to honor and respect you. If they desire to honor and respect themselves, they will not accept benefit packages without honing respective titles. Respectful people do not allow people to take advantage of them, and they do not take advantage of other people. If they do not honor and respect you then they do not truly love you.

If they don't honor and respect themselves, then they truly do not love themselves. If they want to honor and respect themselves, they will not take on responsibilities without benefits that fit their title. If

Love of Life

someone only wants all the benefits and does not want the title, they do not want responsibility for your mind, heart, body, and soul. All of which are naturally incorporated when you give someone your all.

      Be responsible for yourself, and be responsible for others. Being responsible entails dating with intention. You should not flirt with or entertain someone's feelings if you are not going to fully satisfy them. It's like dangling a carrot in front of someone who is hungry and lifting it away from them. It's not funny or fun for the hungry person; it is just cruel. Telling someone you want to use them for their body does not excuse your actions. Being upfront with your intent when it is not in God's will is not respectful, it's just honest.

      Expecting benefits without responsibility will create a master/slave dynamic. If you feel like you're the boss then the other is an interviewee, visitor, or employee. They have to respond and answer to you, and you do not have to answer to them. When two potential partners date they meet up; it is not a one-sided interview. Master/slave dynamics builds obsession by virtue of false justifications based on false beliefs.

      If someone pays $20,000 for an item only to find out it is worth $2.00, they may still have a hard time throwing it away due to the amount they invested. A lot of people will find a way to go back to the fantasy that

Relationships Are Like Jobs

the $2.00 item was worth $20,000. They will try to add zeroes to the $2.00 but it will not fit the bill and it will be a counterfeit. This will require more effort and more loss. Not owning up to the truth is a losing game. Some people have a hard time breaking that reality, and due to embarrassment try to make fantasy true. It's lowly behavior, and one should always choose prowess over cowardice. Walk-in truth, for lies will create more debt. Pay now while you can or you will surely accrue interest at a rate that will make you wish you had paid it off.

Just because someone works at their job for a long time doesn't mean they are happy and fulfilled. It could mean they are comfortable, but it may mean they are trapped but are unmotivated to change jobs. It's a myth that every single person who desires you will show interest. It is also a myth that all investors love who they are invested in. Not everyone who is interested invests and not all investors are invested because they love you.

Stalkers are all investors, and secret admirers may be good at keeping their love a secret. Both are evidently living a lie in terms of showing love. It is important not to assume everyone who invests truly cares for the right reasons, and that everyone who is interested will automatically invest. It is ideal to have all in one but some people are mismatched. The mismatch can be due to maturity, courage, timing, or cognitive dissonance (which

Love of Life

is the state of having inconsistent thoughts, ideas, beliefs, or values).

A lot of people may advise to, "go after someone who invests" and narcissists are good at advertisers for "investment assurance." The assurance is not currency for love unless their interest stems from true love. Not everyone who is interested in you is going to invest; they may never invest. What matters is what is true, and what will actually be. Seek the truth and don't follow assumptions without evidence or else you will miss your opportunity to learn proper lessons.

Just like jobs, not everyone is listed on the market. The highly sought-after positions may not be listed. The next person who dates the one highly sought-after will likely be someone whose presence was known before the previous partner left. Often times, they are regularly receiving applications before the position was open to the public. Sometimes there is an overlap in terms of filling parts of the position while someone else is still in the partnership position. Waiting till someone is fully available and ready may be too late. There usually is a waitlist of people queued for their turn as interviewees, aggressive volunteers, and sneaky appeasers whom you had no idea were in the running.

As long as neither of you are married, let them know you are interested and if they end up leaving the person they are with; note their character and how they went about the transition. There is a reason why some people go from relationship to relationship. When a position opens it's easier to fill it with someone whom you have familiarized yourself with as a possibility. Approximately eighty percent of married people met their spouse when they were already boyfriend/girlfriend with someone else.

Adultery refers to married couples and not boyfriend/girlfriend situations. When going to a wedding and the woman throws her bouquet, women who have boyfriends are still counted as single and therefore eligible to catch the bouquet. Men are too considered single if not married and can catch the garter belt. Nobody is officially yours until you marry them. It is not recommended to date for more than three months before becoming boyfriend and girlfriend.

Most mature men who are seriously looking to get married know within six months (at max a year) of being boyfriend and girlfriend or less if they want to marry the woman they are with. Most happy, healthy fulfilling marriages that last tend to have recognized each other as the one quite quickly or at least within 6 months of courtship. Any recognition after that, you run the risk of just settling. In being settled, one may tell themselves false stories to justify their poor decisions and actions.

Love of Life

Most healthy happy marriages that last and are fruitful did not take more than six months to recognize each other as the one. When one loses faith in what they want, they do whatever whenever. Remember titles say how much you honor the person, just because you have benefits doesn't mean they honor you. Having benefits does not change what the title means, it just makes the title not appear to have meaning.

When one says, "titles do not mean anything," it means there are no guidelines and you are running the risk of dishonor and disrespect. Once you establish a schedule, there will be expectations whether one likes it or not, title or not. The guidelines will be hazy because there are no titles that help one identify responsibilities or benefits. No titles leave room for manipulation, without grounds for responsibility. For example, when arguing one can say, "I never said you were my girlfriend so you cannot expect that from me," or "you are not my husband."

Meaning is important because it is the driving force in life. If you are not driving then you are potentially lost, or complacent, which is a sign you have given up and settled. You haven't arrived, you are on hold and may never arrive. The unhealthy stronghold can hold you back from true love. It is not recommended to give anyone more than half a year if you do not see a future with them as your partner. Time is an investment you

Relationships Are Like Jobs

cannot get back. If you don't know if you want to be with someone and you feel you've thoroughly gotten to know them, then the answer is no, they are not the one for you. Think about anything you truly want in this life; you do not put it off, and if you do put it off, it is because your life is out of order, and if you truly want something you will put your life in order to get it.

It is wise to understand the different ways people handle breakups. Psychologically, breakups can be harder than handling the death of loved ones. Part of the reason is that you still have to live with the loss of someone you can still interact with. Emotionally, heartbreak can cause your health to deteriorate at an alarming rate. It may leave you mentally exhausted, physically drained. What once were butterflies in your stomach feels like empty pits of despair.

Like any other business, when it fails it typically hurts both sides. Most of the time, women are the ones to end relationships verbally, however, men are usually the ones to end relationships emotionally. Both conclusions can be exuded in immature ways.

A boy can emotionally disengage and still engage physically; a girl may physically disengage and may emotionally still engage. When a boy is done with a relationship, he is more likely to neglect his position to satisfy her emotionally. The girl will complain about things he needs to fix, while the boy will simply not fix them. She may break up with him and then be upset to see that he fixed all she complained about with a new woman. If someone has decided in their heart you are not the right one, they will not be motivated to do the right things for the relationship. When the girl is done with a relationship, she is more likely to disengage physically which will force a verbal confrontation that will likely end the relationship. A boy may confront a girl about her physical disengagement and she may give a hazy explanation if she is not ready to break up yet.

    A physical confrontation to end the relationship is more likely to happen before a verbal one. A boy would rather get fired, while a girl would rather quit. To end the relationship, the boy will think of ways to get fired, while the girl will think of ways to quit. If a man believes a woman is the one, he will never leave her. If a man leaves a woman and returns to marry her, he likely gave up on finding his better half, and thought the last woman was the best he could do.

    Men are more likely to keep help or get more help then to get rid of their only help. When women think a man is the one, she may still leave him. If she accepts his return, he could still be the one and the relationship could be repaired. Women are helpmates and if there is no one to help they may leave. It doesn't say in the Bible that it is not good that a woman should be alone. Biblically speaking men are supposed to be leaders and women

Relationships Are Like Jobs

are helpers, the way we orchestrate our roles matters in how we process and think about relationships. If a breakup changes who you are, then your identity was rooted in that person in an unhealthy way.

"Then the LORD God said, "It is not good that the man should be alone; I will make him a helper as his partner."
(Genesis 2:18)

Is it easier to leave a leader or to leave a helper? There is a reason why women are keen to say "leave" and men are more likely to say "let go of" when a relationship has gone sour. Do you leave a helper or get rid of one? Getting rid of someone sounds harsher than leaving someone. If a relationship is a ship and men are the leaders, they are going to kick the woman off the ship, while women will leave the ship to end the relationship with the man. Either one may abandon ship altogether. If a leader Is a bad leader one doesn't often think of getting more leaders, you find a new one. However, if one is a bad helper it's easier to think of gaining more helpers.

This is not to say having multiple helpers is the solution, God did not remove multiple ribs from Adam. Getting more helpers will create more pain than it will pleasure and cause damage in the long run. If you use people for your own selfish pleasure you will divert your route away from your higher self. It is more innate for most women to stick to one man. It's easier for women to be faithful because of their design; however, each

individual may have their own programming that is counterintuitive to the average.

You should not think the average is the absolute program for everyone or that the exception is the rule. However, it helps to know what's common and uncommon. A lot of people base things on their experiences and expectations. Not everyone gets caught doing wrong, but God knows and sees everything. There are laws of design that are unchangeable; however, the ruler of the design can fluctuate. Are they ruled by God? Or are they ruled by sin? Laws do not change, rulers do.

Loving someone doesn't entirely prevent cheating. Surrendering to God and obeying him is a stronger source of accountability and faithfulness. One cannot trust someone who doesn't care to obey God; for without clarity of God, we obey our own desires and only worry about being accountable for what others see. Whether someone cheats or not has everything to do with their character and disposition toward love and discipline.

Men typically do not want to say they gave up. It is socially more acceptable for women to say they did. Men are often very mysterious; they don't reveal everything and often take their deepest thoughts to their grave. A woman can say she knows her man better than anyone else, and that same man may silently disagree

Relationships Are Like Jobs

with her. That silence keeps the peace and keeps intact beliefs that will benefit him.

Boys love to get a reaction out of women, and even grown men do this too, but go about it in different ways. They are mystified by a woman's endurance and tolerance and are constantly testing the limits. A woman should implement her standards by how she walks her grounds, and not reveal or expose herself too much. Keeping mystery between each other helps maintain interest in one another. Mystery inspires exploration which adheres to bonding. Men always test limits to see where they can categorize and asses a woman. A woman looks at a man's works and commitment and categorizes him from there.

If a man wants to honor and respect a woman, he will try to fix the problems they face as a couple. If he doesn't respect a woman it could be due to the benefits a woman has given him and/or because of the responsibilities they misuse or refused to adhere to. He also may not respect himself or may hold an inaccurate title. The same goes in reverse for a woman. If a woman does not want the man to give up, she will encourage him and support him. A man will provide solutions if he wants to love a woman, and a woman will nurture growth if she wants to love a man.

If someone truly loves you, they will talk about who you authentically are rather than what you do. They will

say things like "they have this laugh" or "they are unlike anyone I know." If someone is right for you, they will also be good for you. However, just because they are good, doesn't make them right. If the relationship was bad, they will say "I did so much for them" or "they didn't do enough for me". When the question of "what" they did is the focus versus over reflecting on "who" they are to you, then it is highly likely you weren't in love with each other. True love never ends.

Two mature adults will end a relationship when they are done whether they are a male or female. They will take responsibility for themselves. It's sad to say this hardly happens, but when it does, it is between two people who respect one another. If you don't respect, trust, or have any love for a person, it is easier to leave. With titles come responsibilities and anyone who does want to honor a title does not want to be responsible for your heart.

Anyone who does not want to advance in titles doesn't want the responsibilities of the next step. People who ghost others do not want to be responsible. They rather run off rather than reject you. They won't answer phone calls or show up. Ghosting is cruel because it leaves people concerned or confused which prolong their suffering without answers. It is better to send in your resignation; however, if one was never in a partnership, or lived under an independent contract, one should not expect communication of resignation of someone's desire to not continue.

If someone doesn't want to even start a relationship, their behaviors are much like that of someone who is done with a relationship. A woman, will engage a man emotionally and offer no physicality, a man will offer physicality but not want to engage much emotionally. He won't want to text a woman all day; she won't want to cuddle with a man or hold his hand. Many people think if they offer what they are willing to engage with that they will get the other half they need. For example, some women may have sex with a man thinking he will eventually open up emotionally. A man may emotionally engage a woman hoping she may open up sexually. Typically, this method tends to be a waste of time because this is a faulty way of thinking. It assumes too much based on too little. It assumes to reason for their action and not the cause of their action. Don't assume an action in one area will automatically unlock another area. The gatekeeper knows why they are holding back and it is important to investigate the truth, before assuming a solution.

Typically, body language lets the other person know you are interested first, and the verbal is the confirmation. The duration of time from verbal to physical contact can vary based on allowance and desire. If a man's goal is physical in the first place, he will

cut the verbal aspect as quickly as possible and get to the chase. If the woman's goal was only verbal, she will avoid moments and situations with physical contact as long as possible. This is not to say all women who delay do not want something physical. It may mean she wants to know who the person is before they have access, which is wise. Same reasons for men who delay physical behavior. It may be because he wants to honor and respect the woman he has interest in.

One must discern actions based on desire vs allowance. It is important to communicate desire, and it is vital to note the timing when it may be okay to satiate the desire. Knowing the why behind someone's actions is important because people will fill in blanks in their heads. Many people are insecure and will falter to negative thinking. Make all assumptions optimal questions as opposed to conclusions.

It's important to note that emotional cheating and physical cheating have varying degrees of affect. The bible discusses adultery in a marriage as a sin, however, it also mentions we are to stay away from the appearance of evil. Not everyone catches or thinks about emotional cheating, but one can categorize it as an appearance of evil. When people think about cheating, they primarily think of the love language physical touch but the other love languages can be involved as well. It's hard because physical touch is more obvious in terms of

lines being crossed. For example, kissing and having sex with someone who is not your spouse is a clear violation of a marriage. However, friendships have love languages and it may be hard for some people to identify boundaries.

When do the other love languages cross the lines? A woman can have a guy best friend who she spends quality time with and he can feel romantically loved by her. A man can do acts of service for a woman whom he is just friends with, and she can feel romantically loved by him. Both cross the line because romantic love is being satisfied to a degree. Boundaries need to be established with anyone where romantic/sexual attraction is possible. Someone may have feelings for someone else and cheat through their love language that may not be physical touch.

When someone gets cheated on, they may want a play by play what happened. Just like an actual play there are stages. The stages include the following:

- Exposition
- Rising action
- Climax
- Falling action
- Resolution

Love of Life

The exposition sets the scene and that scene starts with a love language. The rising action is where tension is built. Flirtatious people often at times will set the scene to create tension and feel they have done nothing wrong if they do not reach the climax. The flirt may not take their flirtation seriously but their spouse or the person receiving the flirt may disagree. There is harm in playing with people's feelings. It's best to be conscious of this, and be responsible. Some people collect individuals like dolls on a shelf. They may admire you, but play with someone else. Even if you are not romantically interested in the person you are flirting with, the person receiving the flirt may feel they have collected you and not honor or respect the relationship you are in.

If your partner can be on someone else's shelf, they will appear to not belong to you. It will show that your partner does not honor and respect you. Nobody else should have evidence during the duration of your relationship that they belong to someone else. It's best to not even set the scene, because it can become a crime scene. What one considers "just friends" may reveal more when one looks at the benefits. There is no climax without rising action, sometimes titles are mask to fit in society and people don't have what they truly want. Some people see right through the mask and expose it and test it. Don't live your life as a masquerade. Don't mask your partnership. If you want to act solo be solo and don't hurt

others in the process. Be someone who is accountable and respectable.

No contact with potential romantic/sexual interest is the best guard to protect your romantic relationship. No contact includes words of affirmation, gifts, and other love languages. Keep in mind, someone's giving love language can be words of affirmation and they can utilize it to put other potential relationships on hold. Nobody is official yours till you marry them, but holds are potentials for wreckage for the future. The destruction may be in the future of your relationship, or you may block your "friends" future because they aren't going to look for love elsewhere if they feel they have it. The voids you fill will keep you still and when you do not progress you may decay. Complacency leads to sloth which is a comfortable silent killer. It does not matter if the interest is only one way. You either compromise your blessings, or you block theirs.

One does not need holds if they have the one that they want to hold on to forever. Nobody wants to compromise "the one" if they know they have the one. If they are unsure, others will always be a possibility. During the engagement period, a couple should discuss their boundaries in a marriage. Each love language should be discussed in terms of appropriateness, honor, and respect concerning boundaries. In a marriage, nobody should entertain other options or put anyone on hold.

Love of Life

People can recover from cheating; however, some types of cheating showcase the relationship is over and not suited for a recovery plan. If a woman cheats physically on her man the relationship is over. The recovery chances are so slim it's likely wasteful in terms of time. If a man cheats emotionally, the relationship he is in also does not have a good chance for recovery.

Typically, women are more selective with whom they would have sex with, than who they would emotionally open up to. Men typically are more selective with who they would open up to, than who they may have sex with. Rarity separates people from the pack and "the one" is not identified as part of the pack. "The one" is an expansion pack, they do not maintain mediocracy or degrade you or degrade themselves. A relationship is your main focus and if you lose focus in a rare area that few should have access to, the relationship is over. It's likely run its course and does not need a to be continued. If your connection is strong, looking and indulging elsewhere is counterintuitive. Man or woman, it doesn't matter. The relationship likely was not adequate to have sustenance to grow and develop; hence the opening to look elsewhere.

Relationships Are Like Jobs

When relationships end one should fill out a report card to keep themselves in check:

Relationship

Their Name: Irrelevant
Their Title: Interviewee (dating but never official), well... more like a visitor, looking back... we never really went on dates.

Their Requirements	*Benefits*
Text all day	Sex twice a week Sleepovers

My Requirements	
Text all day I took them to work I made them dinner I bought a ticket to see them out of town Bought them Christmas presents	

1. What do you wish you received from the relationship? Emotional support.

2. What benefits do you regret agreeing to? Sex

3. Did the requirements match the title? No, looking back, we were not married and yet I did things that should only be done in a marriage.

Love of Life

4. Do the benefits match the title? No... but we were practically boyfriend and girlfriend because I had been doing this for eight months.

5. What is your lesson? I will lead with respect for my soul, over leading with the desire of my body. I will do some soul searching to find out why my spirit leads me to make bad decisions.

6. What is your blessing? That I am no longer with someone who did not honor or respect me. That I can spend time building, rather than destroying myself.

7. Did you find yourself justifying or making excuses when asked about the responsibilities and benefits? Yes...

8. How did the relationship end? They ghosted me.

If the last answer included ghosting continue to the next two following questions.

1. Did you have an independent contract or partnership and can you sanely file a missing person's report? Umm...

2. Did you see them interacting with others live, and when they saw you, did they look at you as if you were the ghost? Well...

Relationships Are Like Jobs

Self-Reflection

Why did I allow someone to treat me like a dead body? Was I dead on arrival? Or did it happen during the course of our relationship? My necromantic romance... my dead beliefs made me want to feel alive through someone else's touch. I felt loved; my love language was abused due to false pretenses I set in my head. I cannot even call it a relationship because the ship never sailed, and yet I feel shipwrecked. I am comatose, they were my lifeline. They didn't cherish my body, and I allowed them to destroy my spirit, compromise my soul, and corrupt my mind. Time to stabilize and create my own independence. An independent life that is worthy of an expansion pact. I will require no dependence. No more fantasy and expecting it to be a reality. Their words were a date rape drug slipped into the drink that I imagined as pure water. I had no idea the depths to which I silently consented. I cannot wait until the hangover is over. I will learn to forgive myself and not be so naïve. Never again.

End Report
Keep in files to see growth or repeated patterns.

Love of Life

People stay in toxic relationships for the same reasons people stay at certain jobs. People do not repeat patterns unless they are a habit or there is some sort of pay off. They may feel they need the benefits and may be addicted to the rewards of the job. They may simply just love the title and don't feel good about getting a title elsewhere. They may just be comfortable, don't like trying new things, and are in denial that they are in the wrong place. Whatever the reason, it all comes down to being disconnected from your purpose and motivated by a false sense of security.

Sometimes people will project images of things desired but never have the intention of giving it to you. Think of what you want in life like a GPS map to which you have pinned a destination. If the person you are involved with doesn't give you directions and an estimated time of arrival, do not take them seriously. If they pass the reasonable ETA and you see no traffic or accidents on the way, do not have blind faith in their desire and ability to get you where you need to go. Also, if you are directing someone and they don't want to push the pedal don't expect to get anywhere.

Every man and every woman should have an estimated time for their destination; set your limit before you are given one and see if you can negotiate together. Not setting a time or picking a direction, is choosing to waste your time. You might as well call that person your

Relationships Are Like Jobs

resting place, a comfort zone that is a silent killer. If you are not living you are slowly dying. It's a bad idea to just drive without a target place when it comes to being with someone else. Leave your wondering to rogue missions unless you both have a ventured interest in a set location. Some people get so caught up in the appearances of "going somewhere" that they sabotage themselves.

It's important to note that you may always look insane if you expect requirements that do not match someone's title. You may also look insane offering and solidifying benefits to people who do not have titles or have spent enough time in a particular position. Imagine hiring someone for work and telling them that they can immediately go on vacation, and not have a return to work date. Two insane people can agree that an insane thing is sane.

Date with Intention, or you are playing with people's hearts. It has consequences even if two people are in agreeance. Not everyone is in their right mind when indulging people. If you have to make excuses then you likely made assumptions. Don't make assumptions. Seek good, guard against evil. Put God at the center of all you do. When you take benefits and fulfill the requirements of a partnership to nurture your partner's mind, body, spirit, and soul and then you chose not to marry them you are choosing not to honor God, yourself, or that other person. When you give someone a title, you honor them. Saying

Love of Life

the title doesn't matter is also saying it doesn't matter is that you honor yourself or your partner.

     Jewels lack currency if it spread around and given to anyone without work, title, or requirements. Without work, a relationship is just play, and you and your partner toys. You are playing house, and a mature adult should have no time for such child's play. Keep in mind what you are doing with your time, it is an investment no matter how you label it.

     Use your time intentionally; it's no fun to have a bunch of memories with people you wish you did not invest your time in. Creating memories with someone is time you are investing in them, and if you do not want to treasure them you are wasting time. God's time is his time, and his will is his way, and if you want to see the way and live his will do not allow distractions to lead you into being blind on a crooked path. Mistakes are common but we don't want to do them intently and frequently.

     Always do your best. Relationships are not perfect but they are not supposed to be an arduous job with you wrecked as a person. If problems cannot be addressed, then they will become cancerous. Depending on what stage you found cancer in your relationship, it indicates the potential for survival. If nobody wants to deal with or acknowledge the real issues, then you have a real

Relationships Are Like Jobs

problem that will kill the relationship. Do not go with the flow of whatever blows your way, be the momentum that

causes the wind that coincides with purpose. How do we know whether to end a relationship? If you started it and God didn't send them. When you do not wait on God, you will end up with counterfeits. End things quickly, intentionally, and trust in God.

> "Trust in the Lord with all your heart, and do not rely on our own insight. In all your ways acknowledge him, and he will make straight your paths."
> (Proverbs 3:5)

Kingdom Discernment

Fantasy & Reality

"Do not be conformed to this world, but be transformed by the renewing of your minds, so that you may discern what is the will of God – what is good and acceptable and perfect."
(Romans 12-2)

In order to discern things as true or false, we must use our senses. We have seven senses, Sight, Smell, Taste, Hearing, Touch, Vestibular (balance), and Proprioception (positioning). It is through these vessels we gain clarity of discernment as we build our self-esteem.

"See, I am sending you out like sheep into the midst of wolves; so be wise as serpents and innocent as doves."
(Matthew 10:16)

Here are the 7 tools of Discernment:

Walk in Faith and Not Fear of Culture (Sight)

Rescue Dog and Sitting Duck Syndrome (Vestibular)

Tales from the Negaverse (Hear)

Do You Love Who You Have to Be? (Touch)

What, When, Why How? (Taste)

Tax Return Love (Proprioception)

The Roses (Smell)

Walk in Faith and Not Fear of Culture

(Sight)

"Set your minds on things that are above, not on things that are on earth."
(Colossians 3:2)

Faith is the opposite of sight. Set your sights on the Kingdom of God. Culture teaches us what we commonly see. In being common, we compare ourselves to everyone else. The Kingdom teaches us righteousness. Culture creates its own set of rules based on the feeling of the time. There is culture's way, and culture's timing and it may not resonate with God's timing, God's will, and God's way.

Culture's way and timing can incite fear into those whose timeline does not resonate with the average person. Care about the opinion of God, not the culture. We are meant to live our lives authentically and in heavenly harmony. It is our life song, and it can be defined by any length of time, beat in tempo, high or low frequency, or volume. If you are living someone else's

Love of Life

song then you will be living in deception, this is not the will of the Lord.

"Not everyone who says to me, 'Lord, Lord,' will enter the kingdom of heaven, but only the one who does the will of my father in heaven. On that day many will say to me, "Lord, Lord, did we not prophesy in your name, and cast out demons in your name, and do many deeds of power in your name?" Then I will declare to them, "I never knew you; go away from me you evildoers."
(Matthew 7:21)

Walk in Faith and Not Fear of Culture

Entertainment culture has a hierarchy of needs of success. Pride is heavily valued. Pride sustains itself by greed, which begets envy, and turns into lust addictively, then transfers quickly into gluttony, which burns into wrath to the point to where one is exhausted and goes into sloth. The sloth has no energy yet is the bottom of the pyramid. It holds the possibility of someone with pride to stay on top. The sloth will relentlessly watch the person with pride, and envy them.

Culture's needs are a pyramid scheme, and it will not fulfill you. We are to serve God, not the culture. Pride is at the top; sloth is at the bottom. Acts of Service is abused when pride and sloth are in battle. Note how pride and sloth are soul-based. In the pyramid scheme of

Love of Life

culture, they want your soul to conform. All the other sins lie in between them, sustaining narcissism on top. God is supposed to be on top of everything we do, not our own pride. There isn't enough shame around sloth in culture, but it allows all the other sins to be free to rule.

> *"I urge you, brothers and sisters, to keep an eye on those who cause dissensions and offenses, in opposition to the searching that you have learned; avoid them. For such people do not serve our Lord Christ, but their own appetites, and by smooth talk and flattery they deceive the hearts of the simple-minded."*
> *(Romans 16:1-18)*

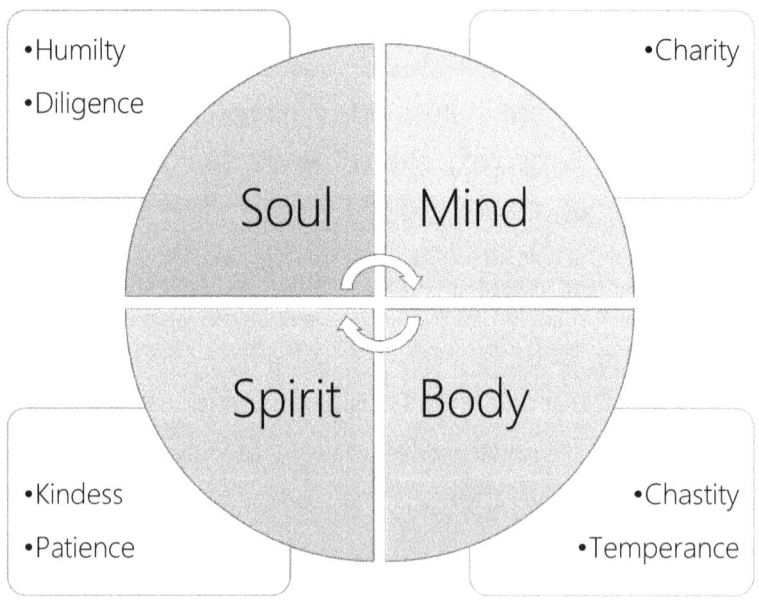

Walk in Faith and Not Fear of Culture

"Peace I leave with you; my peace I give you. I do not give to you as the world gives. Do not let your hearts be troubled, and do not let them be afraid."
(John 14:27)

Kingdom renews, nourishes, and balances. It is connected to a healthy and functioning life. Morals are principles that do not change despite what culture says. Culture shifts; Kingdom doesn't shift.

Now faith is the assurance of things hoped for, the conviction of things not seen.
For we walk by faith, not by sight.
(Hebrews 11:1) (2 Corinthians 5:7)

Leading by sight can be deceiving. Hopelessness is a surrender to your ability to see good possibilities. Faith is hope in fruits not yet seen.

"The eye is the lamp of the body. So if your eye is healthy, your whole body will be full of light, but if your eye is unhealthy, your whole body will be full of darkness. If then the light in you is darkness, how great is the darkness!"
(Matthew 6:22)

People who are governed by their vices become parasites and a virtuous person who does not have discernment will inevitably host them. Helping people is a good virtue, but boundaries need to be established. If you cannot help someone without hurting yourself in the

Love of Life

process **don't do it**. Shame is a good indicator of loss of light to the darkness. Here is a question to ask yourself,

Am I ashamed to tell people what is going on because they would judge me and or them? Am I afraid to leave out of fear rather than love for that person? If you think of leaving a friend or a partnership and your primary thoughts are about how you will hurt them, rather than miss them, then you are a prisoner of your own fantasy. We all have sinned, but how long must we pay for it? Forgive yourself, let go, and let God.

"Therefore, since we are justified by faith, we have peace with God through -our Lord Jesus Christ, through whom we have obtained access to his grace in which we stand; and we boast in our sufferings, knowing that suffering produces endurance, and endurance produces character, and character produces hope, and hope does not disappoint us, because God's love has been poured into our hearts through the Holy Spirit that has been given to us."
(Romans 5:1-7)

Rescue Dog and Sitting Duck Syndrome

(Vestibular: Maintaining balance in virtue with oneself and another)

"For freedom Christ has set us free. Stand firm, therefore, and do not submit again to a yoke of slavery."
(Galatians 5:1)

Rescue Dog Syndrome

You may be kind to everyone, but you are not to take everyone in. A rescue dog's favorite love language is Acts of Service. They are withered individuals riddled with bad habits. They want you to nurture them to be better health. In that nurturing you will build a bond with that person that feels special and unique. Gaining pity is a stronghold that manipulative people use to gain power. One can look at the sick one as weak, but they gain strength in those who cater to them.

A bond created from tragedy can turn into a "beautiful" savior mission. The sick person appears grateful. Then one day you go out and you run into another person. They are perfectly fit for you in every way - personality, light, discipline, all aligned with your authentic self. You come home and the person you rescued sniffs out that you found a better match. They

Love of Life

yell at you "How can you do this to me? You know what I've been through! You cannot replace me!" Being the

good person that you are, you apologize and claim to never look at another person again. This is a trap a many people fall into, and it does not help you rise to grace. A once heroic position becomes a slave position. The owner is now being owned. Position with Christ.

> *"You were bought with a price; do not become slaves of human masters. In whatever condition you were called brothers and sisters, there remain with God."*
> *(1 Corinthians 7:23-24)*

    Rescue Dogs are typically male, though every man and woman have a canine tendencies inside of them. Like a gene, these must be activated. Dog tendencies include lack of discipline, which stems from immaturity. Pouting, sadness, shame, and guilt may be part of the recipe that keeps a couple together. Pity is usually better targeted at women due to their helping nature. A woman who is unhealthy in her virtue of charity, is likely attract a rescue dog. If gifts is your love language be prepared for rescue dogs to pounce on you and wait for you to throw them a treat.

    If you activate the dog, you will be the owner or you will get owned. This is the typical formula for a covert narcissist also known as a vulnerable narcissist. to be rescued from the stronghold they created with you.

Rescue Dog and Sitting Duck Syndrome

"Do not give what is holy to dogs; and do not throw your pearls before swine, or they will trample them underfoot and turn and maul you."
(Matthew 7:6)

Sitting Duck Syndrome

Women have a higher tendency to be a sitting duck. This syndrome is feminine in its execution. Sitting Duck Syndrome is characterized by someone drowning out their competition to gain success. Sitting ducks are likely to operate in the Quality Time love language, and bond with people who have an unhealthy form of the temperance as their virtue. A man is the most susceptible target for a sitting duck. As a leader, a man may be direct and hunt for what they desire. Women, however, are always told to let a man hunt yet woman are not always told what to do to be noticed.

Since women are helpers, some may think the best course of action is to get all the other ducks in a row. Afterwards, like a duck, they will help themselves by drowning each duck around them. They may eliminate competition through lies, manipulations, and unfair power plays. A sitting duck may lie to the other ducks about the hunter so that the ducks go to another pond. Whatever it takes for the pond to stay clear and highlight the one duck owning the pond. It is calculated and evil and not every hunter will be aware of this tactic if the

work is done before he identifies the serial killing duck as a target for desire.

Both rescue dogs and sitting ducks are indirect hunters. Although sitting duck is feminine in its approach and is a toxic form of "help." They are both covert and yet tactically different. There's eliminating people to hire (Sitting Duck Syndrome tactic), and eliminating people to work for (Rescue Dog Syndrome tactic). A rescue dog may use control by utilizing pity to make you feel uncomfortable about leaving them. After all who gives up a rescue dog? A sitting duck may master you due to their ability to control the environment. Afterall, who else are you going to choose?

You should not use pity or pain to capture someone. The tactical effort of a rescue dog is shameful. A man should use honor, not pity, to capture a woman. A man's honor is based in his character and his character is shown in his works. A woman should not use process of elimination to allure a man. She should use her grace and not disgrace her competition. A woman should not eliminate her competition - she should elevate herself, and let her light speak for itself. A woman can operate as a rescue dog, and a man can orchestrate himself as a sitting duck. Either way they are toxic and confused people.

Rescue Dog and Sitting Duck Syndrome

If you cannot see an option, you are stuck. If you feel you have no choice, you are trapped. Sitting ducks maintain the scale one-to-one by eliminating possible contract options; rescue dogs maintain one-to-one by contract obligation. To end rescue dog syndrome, one will have to break the contract; to end sitting duck syndrome one must seek to find others outside their environment. Both situations require one to break their comfort zone.

It is not noble to be trapped into a relationship whose bond was built on circumstance. Your highest self is your light and is supposed to have an influence, not a consequence. Protect your light over the object of your light. The object of your light, is the person you give your love to. If your light has a consequence, it is an indicator that you may be in the wrong place. If your light must dim in order to be present with someone, then it's a sign that the darkness is claiming the light.

Exalt and illuminate your authentic self and know the difference between building a prison and building a home. If you feel you deserve prison, seek God's forgiveness. If you do not break free, then you will remain broken. A manipulative person will turn the mental prison cell you have in your brain into their hotel room. They will check out when they want to and will come and go as they please. They will make you feel comfortable in a place that you should want to escape. They will make you

Love of Life

feel great about staying where you are, under their rule, and under their control. It may appear to be a pleasurable stay as you await their return, but the room service will cost you a bill that is actually just a bail bond to secure your stay and not your freedom.

Whether you keep the rescue dog in your house, in front of your house, or in your backyard; it will stifle your blessings or block them completely. The sitting duck will keep you blind, and the rescue dog will keep you occupied. Keeping a rescue dog in the front yard seems less personable and therefore less responsible, but it will render you negligent. If it's in your backyard, it appears more responsible; yet still negligent because you are not truly playing house unless you are in the house. Equal playing field is sleeping on the same grounds. If you are not equally yoked and you take them in, you will not be heroic; it will render you pathetic like swine. You will fall prey to illusion seeking validation as a means of wholeness, a nightmarish dream stemming from fear of failure.

Fear of failure is a belief in fragments, but not in wholeness. Love yourself unconditionally to pieces and not only in pieces. Loving yourself in fragments will make it hard for you to piece together a loving identity. If you love yourself to pieces, what will come to be is a better being beyond your imagination. Remember, God's love is unconditional, so do not rely on increments from the

outside world for satisfaction. We are made in God's image and what splits us from God is our lack of belief created by our sinful nature.

Tales from the Negaverse

(Hearing and Perceiving)

"Do not be deceived: "Bad company ruins good morals."

(1 Corinthians 15:33)

After we get hurt, we develop systems to prevent being hurt again. We expect the worst possible scenarios, so we do not get any surprises. DO NOT LET THE ENEMY SPEAK INTO YOUR SPIRIT. One must not forget, that being positive sometimes changes the outcome of the negative reality we were about to face. There may be a one percent chance for goodness in a situation. If there is a chance and it doesn't cost you your authenticity, principles, or wellbeing, it may be worth the effort. Percentages are not guarantees, and all that matters will be the truth and what comes to fruition. This is not to say we overrule a negative truth by being positive. Sometimes, by being positive we give permission to evil.

Love of Life

Example: Let's say you are dating someone who constantly yells at you and calls you an idiot after you did something "out of order." Let's say the abuser says, "I hate you, you're an idiot" and someone interjects and says, "Hey don't let them speak to you like that." You may excuse it by saying "It's okay we're together, it's their way of saying they care about me." This line of positivity is toxic and enables the abuser to continue their negative behavior and get away with it. Jokes only make sense and are funny if they have some truth to them.

"Again, you have heard that it was said to those of ancient times, 'You shall not swear falsely, but carry out the vows you have made to the lord.' But I say to you Do not swear at all, either by heaven, for it is the throne of God, or by the earth, for it is his footstool, or by Jerusalem, for it is the city of the great King. And do not swear by your head, for you cannot make one hair white or black. Let your word be 'Yes, Yes' or 'No, No;' anything more than this comes from the evil one."
(Matthew 5:33)

It is good not to take yourself too seriously, and to be able to laugh at yourself at times. However, if you are smart being called an idiot is an insult. People who are negative have seven tools for destruction:

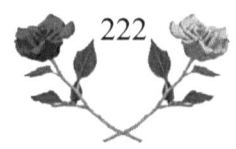

Tales from the Negaverse

Negaverse seven weapons of destruction

Negativity about truth and joy

Positivity towards lies and pain

Spiritual damnation

Limiting beliefs

Temptation instead of inspiration

Confusion

Illusions

"Do not repay evil for evil or abuse for abuse; but, on the contrary, repay with a blessing. It is for this that you were called- that you might inherit a blessing."
(1 Peter 3:9)

Calling you low level names is low-level energy that is immature and unempathetic. The person from the negaverse takes ownership of the negative things you believe about yourself and encouraging it to keep you connected to their lowliness. It is weak, dishonorable, and ultimately wicked.

To trick someone into conditioning that a negative is a positive is incredibly manipulative. If they let it go far

Love of Life

enough, they will end up feeling hopeless and unable to discern a good thing from a bad thing. Which is exactly what a manipulative person wants - you under their control so they can assert their own rules. It will be ruled from the negaverse and it will be deceptive, but once you are under their rule through your permission, you will ultimately be receptive. Once receptive, you may try in a twisted way to redeem yourself by becoming just like them. This is the twisted cycle of the negaverse, to create others like them, and to place those who are not alike under their spell.

The truth is an asset that can aid in your destruction or construction of self. The beauty is that it is a choice what you decide to believe. As Sailor Moon says, "I will right wrongs, and triumph over evil." She acknowledges that there is evil out there, but she believes she has the courage to face it. Have the courage to face evil, but don't seek its company or counsel.

"Do not consult the one who regards you with suspicion; hide your intentions from those who are jealous of you. Do not consult with a woman about her rival or with a coward about war, with a merchant about business or with a buyer about selling, with a miser about generosity or with the merciless about kindness, with an idler about any work or with a seasonal laborer about complete his work, with a lazy servant about a big task—pay no attention to any advice they give. But associate

Tales from the Negaverse

with a godly person whom you know to be a keeper of commandments, who is like-minded with yourself, and who will grieve with you if you fail. And heed the counsel of your own heart, for no one is more faithful to you than it is. For our own mind sometimes keeps us better informed than seven sentinels sitting high on a watchtower. But above all pray to the Most High that he may direct your way in truth."
(Sirach 37:10-15)

Do not seek answers about lions, through the minds of wolves in sheep's clothing. For their corrupted beliefs and ways will lay poison on the fruit of truth, and if believed, will soil and spoil the nutrients of its very essence. You adapt to the world you choose to live in to survive. You should only adopt if you have the strength to influence virtuously and thrive. Energy is highly valuable; it is the constructor or destructor of all things. Where you put your energy reflects what is valuable to you

"For where your treasure is, there your heart will be also."
(Matthew 6:21)

It is VITAL to cease and desist giving energy to destructive forces. It is not fair nor is it right that negative people get more energy than the positive and healthy relationships you could create in your life. What good is it to treasure negativity? It will bury you from the light and proceed to hurt you over and over again. If you construct

Love of Life

a better version of yourself and your "friends" talk badly about you, they aren't really your friend. A good friend is someone you can tell the bad and good news to. If you give them bad news they will listen and empathize with you, not insult you, nor compare themselves or make it about them.

The people who thrive on negaverse energy lure people in with sad stories about themselves and have a twisted sense of justice. Here are the seven characteristics of those people whose energy stems from the negaverse:

7 Signs of Negaverse Behavior

They gossip

They lie

They are cruel to others

They obsess

They are envious

They embellish stories

They are ultimately lazy

Tales from the Negaverse

"Whoever walk with the wise becomes wise, but the companion of fools suffers harm."
(Proverbs 13:20)

Their behavior exudes a low-level frequency and its best to tune out rather than to tune in. They beat people down with their actions, their words, in what they have done, and what they have failed to do. They tend to talk about people being too sensitive instead of taking responsibility for their actions. If you switch the word "they" to "I" and the results resonate with you, consider curving your behavior to be better. Remember the 7 Roars of Conduct - responsibility, review, repent, release, renew, redeem, and rejoice.

If you prick someone with a needle intentionally, it is cruel to say they shouldn't feel it or to just get over it. Telling you to just get over something is a way for you to give permission to their wrongdoings when really, they should be seeking forgiveness if they are a person of good character. A narcissist sees forgiveness as permission and not a means to mercy leading into grace. Don't take anything personally. They will excuse their behavior by asserting their title as friend, girlfriend, boyfriend, husband, or wife. It's best to never allow such people to have these attachments to you. Remember...

Love of Life

"Do not give what is holy to dogs; and do not throw your pearls before swine, or they will trample them underfoot and turn and maul you."
(Matthew 7:6)

The pearls they keep that have your name on it will appear authentic to those who have yet to know you. By giving them these very titles, you give them permission to claim and negate you with "validity". They will appear to treasure you and sell you out.

"A gossip goes about telling secrets, but one who is trustworthy in spirit keeps a confidence."
(Proverbs 11:13)

The Tea on The Negaverse

When it comes to the brand of your character, it is important to preserve it. This entails telling the truth, and not selling other brands of tea (gossip). Your cup of tea should run full. You should not need to quench your thirst with other's tea. You should be brewing your own tea and cultivating it. This does not mean you should isolate yourself from others and never share who you are. Tea parties are fine, just beware who you invite to the table. When you have a tea party, make sure you have your own tea to share, as others share their own. You do not have to share with everyone everything. However, it is

Tales from the Negaverse

wise to be a good consultant and consult others. But above all, consult and seek God first in all things.

Love of Life

"Happy are those who do not follow the advice of the wicked, or take the path that sinners tread, or it in the seat of scoffers; but their delight is in the law of the Lord, and on his law they meditate day and night."

(Psalms 1:1-2)

Questions to identify who may or may not be your cup of tea.

1. What are their values and belief systems?
2. Do they stay true to their principles?
3. Do they have good qualities you possess or would like to possess?
4. Do they help you as well as others?
5. Does their tea nourish or destroy?
6. Is their tea authentic?
7. Are they careless with spilling the tea?

If the dialogue shifts from spilling tea that was leaked from other shops do not fully trust it. Their tea could have mixed with someone else's tea and therefore changed the very properties of the original source. It will be hard to figure out which ingredient disgusted you. Was it a lie or the truth that didn't sit well on your tongue? If

Tales from the Negaverse

your cup of tea is only filled with other people's tea then you suffer from envy and are a sloth in your own works. Always have an identity, and keep in mind those that don't have one.

> *"For I fear that when I come, I may find you not as I wish, and that you may find me not as you wish; I fear that there may perhaps be quarreling, jealous, anger, selfishness, slander, gossip, conceit, and disorder."*
>
> *(2 Corinthians 12:20)*

The negaverse is filled with negativity. You would have to change the very essence of the negaverse from negative to positive. Regardless if you think you are affected by negaverse or not, the subconscious takes downloads. It's best not to have negative clutter from cookies you have stored in the computer that is your mind. Good can only triumph over evil if the strength in energy is stronger than that of evil. It is vital when we look at someone else's power that we do not forget to hone and cultivate our own. The negaverse's power is in shame, guilt, destruction, and titles.

If you learn to be okay with the truth, seek God for forgiveness, the truth will not hold power over you negatively. If you do not give negative people merit to have a title in your life then they will be powerless. If you forget your power or refuse to cultivate it, the negaverse will claim you as their own. What good does their

Love of Life

negativity serve the seven Virtues? It bears no nourishing fruit; however, for the seven Deadly Sins, it does wonders for our destruction. Its fruit produces Lust, Envy, Gluttony, Sloth, Greed, Wrath, and Pride.

> "They are like trees planted by streams of water, which yield their fruit in its season, and their leaves do not wither. In all they do they prosper. The wicked are not so, but are like chaff that the wind drives away. Therefore the wicked will not stand in the judgment, nor sinners in the congregation of the righteous; for the Lord watches over the way of the righteous, but the way of the wicked will perish."
> (Psalms 1:3)

Do You Love Who You Have to Be?

(In touch with self)

"For if any hearers of the word and not doers, they are like those who look at themselves in a mirror; for they look at themselves and, on going away, immediately forget what they are like. But those who look into the perfect law, the law of liberty, and persevere, being not hearers who forget but doers who act— they will be blessed in their doing."
(James 1 23-25)

The cure to low self-esteem is not in receiving compliments and acknowledgment from others, it is wholeness in loving your authenticity. If you do not love who you have to be with someone then they are the wrong person to be with. Love is a choice, and just because we chose someone doesn't mean they are right or good for us. If you are with the right person it will align with God's will and grace. If we do not have self-esteem it's nearly impossible to identify the right people who should be around. It will be virtuously impossible to make the right choices for ourselves. When we do not have self-esteem, we do not recognize ourselves, and therefore do not recognize God's love. If someone is not right in their image in God they are not going to do right by their relationships. God doesn't force His will, but people will force their way and hope God wills it.

> *"The rich is wise in self-esteem, but an intelligent poor person sees through the pose."*
> *(Proverbs 28:11)*

God made each and every one of us unique with different abilities, and personalities. Marry someone who is a compliment to your life and not the center of your life. God should be the center of your life. It is important to be character based and not results based. This is not to say results don't matter because we are to bear fruit, however some fruits take longer than others. When you decide whether to stay or leave a relationship people often ask the wrong questions. Here are some faulty questions and more evolved lines of questioning that can help one discern if they love who they must be.

7 Faulty Lines of Questioning

1. Do I love them? (Love is a choice)
2. Do I want to be with them? (We don't always desire what is right for us)
3. Do they make me happy? (Whose responsibility is that?)
4. Will I ever find someone else who likes me? (Insecurity breeds unnecessary fear)
5. Do they love me? (You can find another person who can)
6. Can I start over? (You can always start over)
7. What will everyone else think of me? (No one else can live your life)

7 Secure Lines of Questioning

1. Are we fulfilled and expanding? (Is the fulfillment one-sided? Is the expansion in a desired mutual direction?)
2. Do I love my identity with this person and is it authentic? (Who do you have to be to

have this person? Do you admire that person? Are you both realistic and actualized?)

3. Am I sacrificing my overall desires in life to secure this relationship? (Are you living your dream or theirs? Do both dreams coincide with one another as one dream or does it smother?)

4. Are they my escape plan, lifeline, or my expansion pack? (When you think of marrying them do you primarily think about leaving your family or the excitement about creating a new one?)

5. Do we nurture each other's vices or virtues? (Are they a liability or an asset? Bad company corrupts good character)

6. When I am not with them, do I have withdrawals? Do I miss them? (If you feel anxious, sick, worried, and obsessive this is an indicator of an unhealthy attachment. Think of a drug addict when they haven't been using, they have trouble focusing and may drop other necessities in order to retrieve a "hit")

7. When in need of help, do I fear they may be angry and selfish or have faith that they will be good and honor me?

"Let love be genuine; hate what is evil, hold fast to what is good; love one another with mutual affection; outdo one another in showing honor. Do not lag in zeal, be ardent in spirit, serve the Lord. Rejoice in hope, be patient in suffering, preserver in prayer."
(Romans 12:9)

You don't want to marry someone who is too similar to you. Picking someone who is at the same level sounds good, however levels change. There is a reason why some marriages end with "we grew apart." You want to be with someone who is chasing to be their higher self. Not everyone has the goal to get to level 7, You may meet someone at level 3 and they may be comfortable there. Look at your goals and look at the climb and be honest with yourself. If you are single go up the latter and don't let anyone weigh you down. If you meet your potential husband or wife help each other, and if they don't want to keep up let them be. If you are married help each other up.

You should have similar values with your partner and your differences should be compatible in a way that keeps your life interesting and challenging in a fruitful way. Besides, God's design for marriage was a leader

helper dynamic. If you are too similar one would have to figure out who is master and who is slave because one or both of you will have to go against your design.

    If you do not find and nourish your purpose, addiction will find you and nurture dependence and distraction. If you do not look up, there will be people you meet on your level that will aid in your comfort. Stalling on your purpose will make you prey and a predator will find you. Lions are predators, and being looked at like a gazelle is not a flattering position. Look at the person you are with, if you can determine who is the predator and who is the prey you do not align with that person fruitfully. The relationship may kill you or that person. A lion and a gazelle can only get along in a plane field for so long. Either the gazelle will become a meal, or the gazelle will escape. Gazelle's are usually shy and cowardly and people will talk to you as if you are one when you are not actualized in your higher self.

    As kids we have a particular palette that adores childish things. Immaturity is linked with lack of empathy. Immaturity stifles true identity, which makes true love impossible. Sometimes due to familiarity people get attached to others as they would their favorite childhood sugary cereal. It isn't a good look when you are a grown adult. As an adult you cannot process bad food the same way and you could when you were younger. You start making adjustments as you feel the consequences of

stuff you once enjoyed. A healthy dish that's balanced and not sugary and addictive becomes more appealing. Healing your life rather than sugar coating it sounds like a better idea after you receive the consequences. Immaturity gets old and stale. Not everyone grows up when they are supposed to. Do you have to stay childish to be with this person? Do you have to be prey? Do you have to compromise the goodness of your character to maintain balance and secure the relationship?

Seek with your eyes and ears open, and make sure you are in touch with the truth; that way you will be able to discern whether the taste of reality satiates your authenticity. Who are you with this person? Is it better or worse? Expansion pack love is the goal. You can both operate individually but together expands a better world for both of you.

"I praise you, for I am fearfully and wonderfully made. Wonderful are your works that I know very well."
(Psalms 139:14)

What, When, Why, How?
(Taste and see. Sweet, Salty, Sour, Bitter)

"Ah, you who call evil good and good evil, who put darkness for light and light for darkness, who put bitter for sweet and sweet for bitter!"
(Isaiah 5:20)

In order to discern truth and its meaning, one must ask these questions. Some people get caught up in one question and miss the bigger picture. Watch and observe people. If you still cannot figure it out, sometimes it's okay to ask. While they answer, study their tone of voice and body language. The top two critical questions are how, and why. Here are some examples featuring different love languages:

Love of Life

Gifts

What did they do? Buy you a gift. (Sweet)

When? It was Valentine's day. (Sweet)

Why? They felt obligated. (Bitter)

How did they get it? They stole it off their co-workers' desk. (Sour)

When you focus on the first question you feel great. However, as you go further into questioning; you feel differently about the action. You have to let things settle before assuming anything. Do not make assumptions.

What, When, Why, How?

Quality Time

What did they do? They took time off work for you. (Sweet)

When? On a Tuesday. (Sweet)

Why? Your ex was flying into town and they felt insecure. (Salty)

How? They spent the last of their sick pay to get the day off. (Bitter)

Some people find when their partner feels insecure that it's a bit flattering. However, this is a way of showing they do not trust you and therefore need to assert control over the situation to reclaim their power. Power struggles are toxic.

Love of Life

Physical Touch

What did they do? They stood on a higher step behind you and put their left hand on your left shoulder as they stood to your right. (Sweet)

When? While you were taking pictures. (Unidentified taste bud leaning towards sour)

Why? To assert dominance. (Sour)

How? It was a light pat on the shoulder that was held somewhat aggressively. (Sour)

    Some people may not mind being dominated. They may even enjoy it, but this indicates the people in the photograph are not be equals. Worthiness is not even a question when coupled with someone you are equally yoked to. If you're not equally yoked one of you is getting choked, and the one that is choked, is the one who has someone else's hand on their shoulder. If there is mutual respect, such a pose would naturally be uncomfortable. Check your photographs and read each other's body language.

What, When, Why, How?

Words of Affirmation

What did they say? I love you. (Sweet)

When? After you smiled at them. (Sweet)

Why? They felt loved at that moment and wanted to please you. (Bittersweet)

How? They said it with fear in their voice. (Sour as in rotten fruit)

"The sated appetite spurns honey, but to a ravenous appetite even the bitter is sweet."
(Proverbs 27:7)

Love is not led by fear. People pleasers are loyal to nobody and lack identity. People pleasures lack willpower, which is why a control freak can will power over them. If someone lacks identity, they don't have the capacity to love you. Love is not led by obligation. Sometimes people say things to "keep the peace". Not everyone behaves appropriately when faced with vulnerability. Fight, flight, or freeze may occur and whatever comes naturally will likely be used. At times, people roll with energies, they live life "any way the wind blows," and they are simply reflecting yourself back to you. It is hard at times for people to reject gifts or other offerings of kindness and desire. Some people live this fantasy for a long time and then are bewildered when

Love of Life

their relationship falls apart. Don't believe the fantasy if it is not in line with reality. It's hard to lie with your body language and tone of voice because one or both will usually tell the truth. It takes a skilled actor to create an illusion, and most people are not good actors.

What, When, Why, How?

Acts of Service

What did they do? Cleaned the clutter in the house. (Sweet)

When? Before you got back from work. (Sweet)

Why? There was too much stuff. (Sweet) (Salty aftertaste)

How? They threw away only your stuff but none of their own. (Sour)

It's important to be fair while being considerate. The why seems sweet at first, but when followed by how it becomes salty. It is good to be clean and not have a lot of clutter. This should be evident in the lives of husband and wife. Your identity is vital and crucial to have a fulfilling life, and if someone robs you of it then you should no longer give them room to claim you as their significant other.

Love of Life

While seeking the truth, don't make assumptions, especially based on the one taste bud you tend to gravitate to. Out of all the questions asked the one that is the hardest to get revealed is "why". It is a question that plagues people and it's best not to get caught in this question for long. Especially when it is in accordance with a psychopath, sociopath, or narcissist. Insanity needs no modes of reason for justification.

"For God is my witness, how I long for all of you with compassion of Christ Jesus. And this is my prayer, that your love may overflow more and more with knowledge and full insight to help you determine what is best so that in the day of Christ you may be pure and blameless, having produced the harvest of righteousness that comes through Jesus Christ for the glory and praise of God."
(II Philippians 1:8-11)

Tax Return Love

(Proprioception: Awareness in position of oneself with another)

"But the tax collector, standing far off, would not even look up to heaven, but was beating his breast and saying, 'God, be merciful to me, a sinner!'"
(Luke 18:13)

Inconsistent rewards breed unhealthy attachments. The uncertainty will drive you mad, and the reward will make you settle into no longer complaining. It is a formula to build on obsession and regression into falling short of God's grace. Who is giving you tax return love? You work all year giving your all only to be returned a portion of what you've done. Those who celebrate their tax return check don't know their worth.

It can be tricky at times; someone can emotionally abuse you without you knowing it consciously. They can give you permission without room for allowance. It could be as simple as someone saying, "Go out with your friends, I want you to have freedom" and then they text you the whole time. They can also fake emergencies, and fake urgencies for you to return home. You will be so anxious to being away from them, that you will no longer enjoy going out. And stay with them. It can be confusing, and emotionally debilitating.

Love of Life

No individual should govern you. They should add to your life regularly, not take from it and "reward" it sporadically. Love is not supposed to be a taxing experience. You shouldn't be in a position to be collected. If someone is taxing you for your past it's time to end it. If they cannot forgive you and show you mercy for a past transgression it's best to cut the losses and sever the relationship. People who do not have patience, should not be in relationships. Changed behavior and not wasting what is given should suffice.

Anxiety is a symptom of something being out of sync with the truth and or harmony of goodness. Some experiences change people and it doesn't make sense to return to the same relationship because it no longer exists. If you resent who you are, or who you were with someone, chances are that relationship was a lesson. If constant anxiety and unforgiveness are present without improvement, it's best to move forward with someone else. Once someone must punish you to deserve or earn you again it's toxic. Best to start a clean slate with someone who has nothing to "forget" and nothing to "forgive" as you become a better person.

Example: Tax Return Love. Let's say Acts of service is your love language, and you frequently administer it to your significant other and get exhausted and drained. In return you receive a gift as their love language to you, only it wasn't taxing for them to give it at all. You have a

person trying to be worthy, while the other person already thinks of their own self as worthy. You may have chosen to deduct taxes from your check; however, it is wrong for them to accept it. Their belief that they don't owe you anything is true, because love is debt-free. You are supposed to grow in emotional wealth together not depreciate in value. The belief that you owe them something is false. It comes from a lack of something you are trying to overcompensate for. An illusion that was manmade and not divine from God. It's bad to adhere to such illusions, and it's bad that they assisted in creating it into a reality.

Take responsibility, and question the manipulator's motives and integrity. The partner without tax deduction is taking advantage of your delusion, and that intent is driven by selfishness. They don't love you enough to do right by you even when you do wrong to yourself. They will let you fall short and miss your mark, to sin and fall from grace. This is a red flag. The devil is prideful and will wear that red flag as a cape. They will pretend to aid you by barely underserving you to make you feel better about your investment in a toxic cycle. Don't be impressed, don't seek vengeance for it is a losing game. Seek discernment and spend your time fruitfully. Don't take anything personally.

Love of Life

  Tax Return Love elicits what is called the D.E.N.N.I.S System which is featured in the show It's Always Sunny in Philadelphia: Season 5, Episode 10.

Demonstrate Value

Engage Physically

Nurture Dependence

Neglect Emotionally

Inspire Hope

Separate Entirely

  When one looks at past relationships one should figure out the formula that got them addicted. Some people stay at the "Inspire Hope" portion of the D.E.N.N.I.S system and don't separate. They stay committed to fantasy. Or they are stuck at the neglect emotionally stage. If one does not engage physically it will be hard to nurture dependence, however, one can nurture dependence by being engaged emotionally. Rescue dogs are exceptional at being emotional tax collectors. Their deceits are so covert that yearly an individual can end up owing and paying for years. They will pay for years due to an unreleased of assets one did not know they acquired. The things you own can end up owning you. The taxes you can owe on that relationship can ruin you for a lifetime.

The Roses
(Smell)

"Instead of perfume there will be a stench; and instead of a sash, a rope; and instead of well-set hair, baldness, and instead of a rich robe, a binding sackcloth; instead of beauty, shame."
(Isaiah 3:24)

We acclimate to the smell of our surroundings. Sometimes we must remove ourselves and return to experience the scent as it is and not how we once perceived it. Real roses have a scent and you must have knowledge of what that is. Some people were raised around fake roses and have had minimal or no exposure to real roses. Your parents will be the closest markers to influence your thoughts on love. Even if they were absent your whole life it still has an effect. Fake roses may have no scent or a manufactured scent to trick you.

"Perfume and incense make the heart glad, but the soul is torn by trouble."
(Proverbs 27:9)

An authentic rose represents real happiness. An inauthentic rose represents fake happiness. If the scent is coming from a manufactured place, it will not nourish you. Your mind may be tricked by the placebo effect but

Love of Life

your body will tell you the truth. Others that enter the room may tell the truth as well because they have just freshly entered and have not habituated to the scent. A toxic person will teach their victims to habituate to the scent they create, to induce a new belief system, and baseline to master their victim's mind, body, spirit, and soul. This is why a toxic person would prefer to isolate their victims. But *People with a good sense of smell may enter sniff out their wickedness and destroy the very world they created to imprison you.*

    The best means of attaining clarity is to leave for a time, heal yourself (during this period of time you should not make contact or it will interfere with clarity) and then discern if you would like to return. Upon arrival, if you so choose, you will notice the scent or lack of scent. It may smell like trash or like roses, or a combination of different things. Notice the effects on your body when you leave. Is it anxious? Does it feel healthier? Anxiousness is a bad sign. Anything resembling a drug-like withdrawal shows you had an unhealthy attachment. The withdrawal period can be so bad that people think the remedy is to return.

    Upon return, one may adore the familiar scent however; the taste may not be how one remembered. Either you changed or they changed during that period of time. Sometimes something feels good because it's familiar and not necessarily because it's good. The cheap

The Roses

imitation of something real seems satisfying; it will look good when others enter the room. An empty room can look like an insane asylum to some, which is why people tend to occupy themselves in a relationship regardless of whether it is with the wrong person or not. Being single for some people is like being homeless, and choosing to go to prison (bad relationship) is an immediate solution to finding shelter.

If you have a scarcity mindset you will likely end up with less than the best you could have. Culture's way of thinking, and is not God's way of thinking. It's better to be alone and at peace than to be with the wrong person. Love is not an obligation to a false reality. *You will never recover the lost time spent with the wrong person; it is better to end it sooner rather than later.* Who is more fruitful of your time? The bad or the good people? Either way, you pay but there is nothing better than looking forward to the fruits of a tree you want to plant.

Do not water for the culture, water for the fruit that enriches your soul. Some people are good at detecting fake flowers and will blow the cover of your fantasy once they smell the roses. Be impeccable with your word. Always do your best. Opposites attract and complement each other. It could be good or bad relationship. If you believe a lie (you believe the fake rose is real) and if the liar enables that belief you are a match, just not a good

Love of Life

one. It is a fantastical life, and you will pay with reality. Are you watering fake roses?

Conclusion

"The wicked flee when no one pursues, but the righteous are as bold as a lion."
(Proverbs 28:1)

What makes a lion and its lioness so captivating? Their very essence commands respect. It does not take a pride of lions to speak for the multitude of its own individual excellence. It is in their serenity and strength that makes them captivatingly beautiful. In loving life, we do not freeze, we take flight, and we fight.

Flight

"Correcting opponents with gentleness. God may perhaps grant that they will repent and come to know truth, and that they may escape from the snare of the devil, having been held captive by him to do his will."
(2 Timothy 2:25-26)

Fight

"Take the helmet of salvation, and the sword of the Spirit, which is the word of God."
(Ephesians 6:17)

We fight with honor, and with grace. A life well-loved and respected. Being a lover and not a fighter is selfless; being a fighter and not a lover is cowardice. It is in being a lover and a fighter that we thrive, and not only survive. Love life the Kingdom way, with no illusions from culture, or made-up rules to satisfy our sinful nature without judgment. Lies and illusions are contusions on the mind and corrupt the spirit. A sober mind, a pure heart, a healthy body, and a joyful spirit stem from the truth of our authentic soul, and there is no illusion that can compensate for that reality.

Questions to ask Oneself

1. Is there a place where I have sacrificed my authenticity because of someone else's feelings and therefore violated my own principles?

2. How can I commit to faith over fear so that the result doesn't corrupt my principles and repress my authenticity?

3. Do my actions involve loving or hating my authentic self through vices and virtues?

4. Do my actions connect me or disconnect me from my purpose?

5. Who hurt me? And what false lesson did I learn that did not empower me? How would you like to challenge it?

6. Is the company I keep reaping what I ought to sow? If not, are we complimenting or destroying each other?

7. What is the first starting step to a goal I can impeccably accomplish to start a better version of self?

Ogeyi is a creative artist whose name translates to "More than the eye can see". She is a writer, life coach, and stylish mystery woman. She believes life should be lived like a movie; "It may not always be happy, but it better be good and authentic."

www.ogeyi.com

www.ingramcontent.com/pod-product-compliance
Lightning Source LLC
Chambersburg PA
CBHW071426150426
43191CB00008B/1056